This synoptic essay considers the nature and evolution of the Marxist theory that developed in Western Europe, after the defeat of the proletarian rebellions in the West and the isolation of the Russian Revolution in the East in the early 1920s. It focuses particularly on the work of Lukács, Korsch and Gramsci; Adorno, Marcuse and Benjamin; Sartre and Althusser; and Della Volpe and Colletti, together with other figures within Western Marxism from 1920 to 1975. The theoretical production of each of these thinkers is related simultaneously to the practical fate of working-class struggles and to the cultural mutations of bourgeois thought in their time. The philosophical antecedents of the various schools within this tradition—Lukácsian, Gramscian, Frankfurt, Sartrean, Althusserian and Della Volpean—are compared, and the specific innovations of their respective systems surveyed. The structural unity of 'Western Marxism', beyond the diversity of its individual thinkers, is then assessed, in a balance-sheet that contrasts its heritage with the tradition of 'classical' Marxism that preceded it, and with the commanding problems which will confront any historical materialism to succeed it.

Perry Anderson

Verso

Considerations on
Western Marxism

First published by NLB, 1976
© Perry Anderson, 1976

Verso Edition first published 1979
© Perry Anderson, 1979
Second impression, 1984
Third impression, 1987

Verso, 15 Greek Street, London W1

Printed in Great Britain by
Thetford Press Limited, Thetford, Norfolk
ISBN: 978-0-86091-720-5

Contents

Foreword

A few words are necessary to explain the occasion and nature of this short text. Written in early 1974, it was designed as an introduction to a collection of essays by various authors on recent theorists of European Marxism. Fortuitously, the educational publishing house which had commissioned this 'reader' ceased to exist a month later. The cancellation of the project deprived the text of its original purpose. These circumstances account for certain of the anomalies of the survey below, if they do not necessarily excuse them. For the essay published here is concerned with the general coordinates of 'Western Marxism' as a common intellectual tradition; it does not contain a specific scrutiny or a comparative evaluation of any of the particular theoretical systems within it. This was to be the province of the studies to which it was a preamble. These were to constitute a series of critical expositions of each of the major schools or theorists of this tradition – from Lukács to Gramsci, Sartre to Althusser, Marcuse to Della Volpe. The present text, focused on the formal structures of the Marxism that developed in the West after the October Revolution, abstains from substantive judgements of the relative merits or qualities of its main representatives. In fact, of course, these have not been equivalent or identical. A historical balance-sheet of the unity of Western Marxism does not preclude the need for discriminating estimates of the diversity of achievements within it. Debate over these, impossible here, is essential and fruitful for the Left.

If, beyond the particular moment of its composition, the text was motivated by more lasting preoccupations, which permit its publication today, it was because it reflected certain problems encountered in the course of work on a socialist journal, *New Left Review*, over the years. An essay written in the late sixties for this review had tried to delimit and analyse a particular configuration of national culture in England since the First World War.[1] One of its principal themes was that English culture had significantly lacked any tradition of 'Western Marxism' in this epoch – an absence registered in an unequivocally negative light. Much of the work of *New Left Review* in this period was devoted to a conscious attempt to start, in some sense, to remedy this native deficiency – by publishing and discussing, often for the first time in Britain, the work of the most salient theorists from Germany, France and Italy. This programme, pursued methodically, was reaching its end by the early seventies. Logically, a concluding balance-sheet of the legacy which the Journal had sought to make available in an organized form, was needed. It was in this perspective that the themes considered here were first evolved. The essay below on a 'continental' tradition from Europe is thus in part a sequel to the earlier account of an 'insular' pattern in England. It was the product of an increasing awareness that the heritage that Britain had missed, to its detriment, was itself missing in certain of the classical traits of historical materialism. A greater equity of judgement, in assessing the national variations and international fate of Marxism in this epoch, was a tacit consequence.

Resuming as it did one of the central concerns of the journal, the text was discussed and criticized by colleagues on *New Left Review*, from a wide range of viewpoints, shortly after the 'reader' for which it had been written was abandoned. In revising the text for publication, I have tried to take account of their reflections and criticisms. I have also emended it where I thought local improvements could be made to its argument, and given references to later developments.[2] The document that remains has been modified as far as its intrinsic form permits. Since its initial composition, however, certain of its emphases now appear to me to pose problems that admit of no ready solution within the text. These misgivings are not amenable to any reworking of the present essay. They are therefore consigned to an afterword which sets out further unanswered questions for any enquiry into the future of historical materialism.

[1] 'Components of the National Culture', *New Left Review*, 50, July–August 1968. Certain elements in this text would be subject to modification today.

[2] Notes in square brackets are those which refer to texts or events subsequent to the writing of the essay.

A decade after its original composition, this essay calls for a few supplementary lines. The collection for which it was initially designed as an introduction appeared as a separate book in 1977, *Western Marxism—A Critical Reader* (NLB), reprinted in 1983 (Verso). That volume, with its detailed studies of individual thinkers, represents the intended companion and control of the general survey attempted here. The essay on Gramsci's theory of hegemony, promised as a more personal pendant to this text, was published in *New Left Review* No 100, November – January 1977, as 'The Antinomies of Antonio Gramsci'. These were the immediate complements to *Considerations on Western Marxism*.

Among the specific reflections with which the text ends was the expectation, and hope, that Marxist history and philosophy would cease to lead such separate lives, and start to meet in a common socialist culture in which each took the challenge and stimulus of the other. The first major occasion of this encounter was the subject of a subsequent book, *Arguments within English Marxism* (1980), which reviews the cumulative work of Edward Thompson, and the significance of its critique of the thought of Louis Althusser. The wider pattern of development of Marxism in the West, since the mid seventies, I have tried to resume in the lectures entitled *In the Tracks of Historical Materialism*, published in 1983—a study that is not quite a sequel to *Considerations on Western Marxism*, since its focus includes currents of thought rival or antagonistic to historical materialism, as well as the fate of Marxism itself. But it does start with the series of forecasts with which the earlier work concludes, and then looks at how the real history, intellectual and political, of the subsequent decade treated them. Many of these predictions, I argue, have been fulfilled; others, significantly, have not. The lectures discuss the directions and reasons of the changes I did not foresee, and in doing so make a number of criticisms of particular judgements, of thinkers or traditions, in the text at hand. For readers interested to pursue my present view of the field, then, *In the Tracks of Historical Materialism* can be read as a continuation of *Considerations on Western Marxism;* or together with *Arguments within English Marxism*, the three studies can be taken as an unpremeditated trilogy. October 1984

Correct revolutionary theory assumes final shape only in close connection with the practical activity of a truly mass and truly revolutionary movement.

LENIN

The multitude, and those of like passions with the multitude, I ask not to read my book; nay, I would rather that they should utterly neglect it, than that they should misinterpret it after their wont.

SPINOZA

The Classical Tradition

The history of Marxism since its birth a little over a hundred years ago has yet to be written. Its development, still relatively brief in span, has nevertheless been complex and displaced. The causes and forms of its successive metamorphoses and transferences remain largely unexplored. The limited subject of the considerations here will be 'Western Marxism', a term that in itself indicates no precise space or time. The aim of this brief essay will therefore be to situate a certain body of theoretical work historically, and to suggest the structural coordinates which define its unity – in other words, that constitute it, despite internal divergences and oppositions, as a common intellectual tradition. To do so involves some initial reference to the prior evolution of Marxism, before the emergence of the theorists in question; for this alone will enable us to see the specific novelty of the pattern they represent. An adequate account of the whole earlier record of historical materialism would, of course, demand much more extensive treatment than is possible here. However, even a summary retrospective sketch will help to bring subsequent shifts into a clearer focus.

The founders of historical materialism, Marx and Engels, were born in the first decade after the Napoleonic Wars. Marx (1818–83) was the son of a lawyer in Trier, Engels (1820–95) of a manufacturer in Barmen: both were Rhinelanders by origin, from prosperous bourgeois backgrounds in the most advanced and westerly regions of Germany. Their life and work, stamped on public memory, need little rehearsal here. It is well known how, under the gravitational pull of the first proletarian upsurges after the industrial revolution, Marx in his twenties progressively settled his accounts with the philosophical legacy of

Hegel and Feuerbach, and the political theory of Proudhon, while Engels discovered the realities of the working-class condition in England and denounced the economic doctrines that legitimated it; how the two wrote the *Communist Manifesto* on the eve of the great continental upheaval of 1848, and fought on the extreme left flank of the international revolts of that year, for the cause of revolutionary socialism; how they were hunted by a victorious counter-revolution into exile in England in their thirties; how Marx drew the historical balance-sheet of the French revolution that had ended in the Second Empire, while Engels summed up that of the failure of the contemporaneous German revolution; how Marx, alone in London, in extreme penury, embarked on the monumental theoretical task of reconstructing the capitalist mode of production as a whole, aided only by the intellectual and material solidarity of Engels in Manchester; how after fifteen years of labour, the first volume of *Capital* was published just before Marx reached the age of fifty; how towards the end of the same period, he participated in the foundation of the First International, and then invested the most intense effort in leading its practical work as an organized socialist movement; how he commemorated the Paris Commune, and instructed the newly unified German workers' party, establishing the general principles of a future proletarian state; how in the last years of Marx's life and after his death, Engels produced the first systematic expositions of historical materialism that made it a popular political force in Europe, and in his seventies presided over the growth of the Second International, in which it became the official doctrine of the major working-class parties of the Continent.

The enormous achievement of these interwoven lives is not our direct concern here. For our purposes, it will be enough to emphasize certain *social* hallmarks of the theoretical work of Marx and Engels, that may serve as a standard of comparison for later developments. Marx and Engels were isolated pioneers within their own generation; no contemporary of any nationality can be said to have fully understood or shared their mature views. At the same time, their work was the product of a long joint endeavour, an intellectual partnership without any close parallel in the history of thought to this day. The two men together – through exile, impoverishment and drudgery – never lost contact with the major struggles of the proletariat of their time, despite their virtually complete lack of any organizational bond with it for over a decade. The depth of the historical connection between the thought of Marx and Engels and the evolution of the working class was best proved by the very ordeal of the years from 1850 onwards, when they were both apparently forced back into 'private' existence: the period was used by Marx, with the constant material aid of Engels, for the preparation of *Capital*, and ended with his natural cooption into the First International, which soon became a practical leadership of it. On the other hand, the extraordinary unity of theory and practice achieved, against all adversities, in the lives of Marx and Engels was by the same token never an unbroken or immediate identity. The single revolutionary upheaval in which they personally participated was predominantly artisan and peasant in its mass character; the tiny German proletariat played only a small role in the events of 1848.[1] The most advanced social insurrection which they witnessed from afar was likewise mainly artisanal in character, the Paris Commune. Its defeat ensured the dissolution of the First International, and the return of Marx and Engels to merely informal political activity once again. The real emergence of industrial working class parties occurred after Marx's death. The relationship between Marx's theory and proletarian practice was thus always uneven and mediate: there was very rarely a direct coincidence between the two. The complexity of the objective articulation between 'class' and 'science' in this period (still virtually unstudied today) was in turn reflected in the nature and fate of Marx's writings themselves. For the limits of the working-class movement of the time set certain boundaries to the work of Marx and Engels. This can be seen at two levels – both in the reception and the scope of their texts. Marx's theoretical influence in the strict sense remained relatively restricted in his own life. The greater bulk of his writings – at least three-quarters of them – lay unpublished when he died: what he had published was scattered haphazardly over a number of countries and languages, without being available as a whole in any of them.[2] It was

---

[1] See Theodore Hamerow, *Restoration, Revolution, Reaction*, Princeton 1958, pp. 137–56: the best historical analysis of the social composition of the German Revolution of 1848.

[2] Among the works unpublished in Marx's own lifetime were: *Critique of Hegel's Philosophy of Right* (1843); *Economic-Philosophic Manuscripts* (1844);

4

to be another half century before all his major works were in the public domain, and the history of their posthumous appearance was to form a central strand in the later vicissitudes of Marxism. The register of Marx's publications in his own time is an index of the barriers to the diffusion of his thought among the class to whom it was addressed. Conversely, however, the inexperience of the proletariat of the epoch – still half-way between workshop and factory, largely devoid even of trade-union organization, without hope of winning power anywhere in Europe – circumscribed the outer limits of Marx's thought itself. Fundamentally, Marx left behind him a coherent and developed *economic* theory of the capitalist mode of production, set out in *Capital*, but no comparable *political* theory of the structures of the bourgeois State, or of the strategy and tactics of revolutionary socialist struggle by a working-class party for its overthrow. At most, he bequeathed a few cryptic anticipations in the 1840s and laconic principles in the 1870s ('dictatorship of the proletariat'), together with his famous conjunctural analyses of the Second Empire. In this respect, Marx's work could not outrun the real historical pace of the masses, in the invention of their own instruments and modalities of self-emancipation. At the same time, and this was a more obvious lacuna to contemporaries, Marx never provided any extended general account of historical materialism as such. This was the task that Engels took up in the late 1870s and 1880s, with the *Anti-Dühring* and its sequels, in response to the growth of new working-class organizations on the continent. For the final paradox of the historical relationship of the theoretical work of Marx and Engels to the practical struggles of the proletariat lay in the distinctive form of its internationalism. Neither man was ever rooted in a national political party after 1848. Based in England, where they remained largely outside the local cultural and political framework, both consciously decided against returning to Germany in the 1860s, when either could have done so. Abstaining from any direct role in the building of national organizations of the working-class in the major industrial countries, they advised and guided militants and leaders throughout Europe and North America. Their correspondence extended effortlessly

---

Theses on Feuerbach (1845); *The German Ideology* (1846); *Grundrisse* (1857–8); *Theories of Surplus-Value* (1862–3); *Capital* Vols II and III; *Critique of the Gotha Programme* (1875); *Notes on Wagner* (1880).

from Moscow to Chicago, and Naples to Oslo. The very narrowness and immaturity of the working-class movement of the epoch permitted them to realize, at a price, a purer internationalism than was to be possible in the next phase of its development.

The group of theorists who succeeded Marx and Engels in the generation after them was still small in number. It was comprised of men who for the most part came to historical materialism relatively late in their personal development. The four major figures of this period were Labriola (born in 1843), Mehring (born in 1846), Kautsky (born in 1854) and Plekhanov (born in 1856).[3] All were from the more backward Eastern or Southern regions of Europe. Mehring was the son of a junker from Pomerania, Plekhanov of a landowner from Tambov, Labriola of a landowner from Campania, Kautsky of a painter from Bohemia. Plekhanov was converted to Marxism, after a decade of clandestine Narodnik activity, in exile in Switzerland in the 1880s; Labriola was an established Hegelian philosopher in Rome, who moved over to Marxism in 1890; Mehring had a long career as a liberal democrat and publicist in Prussia, before joining the German Social-Democratic Party in 1891; Kautsky alone had no pre-Marxist past, entering the workers' movement as a socialist journalist in his early twenties. None of these intellectuals were to play a central role in the leadership of the national parties of their country, but they were all closely integrated into their political and ideological life and held official positions in them, with the exception of Labriola who remained aloof from the foundation of the Italian Socialist Party.[4] Plekhanov, after helping to found the Group for the Emancipation of Labour, was on the first editorial board of *Iskra* and the Central Committee of the Russian Social-Democratic Labour Party elected at its Second Congress. Kautsky was editor of *Die Neue Zeit*, which became the

---

[3] Bernstein (1850–1932), intellectually a minor figure, belonged to the same generation. Morris (1834–96), older than any of this group, was of much greater significance, but unjustly remained without much influence even within his own country, and was unknown outside it.

[4] Labriola had been instrumental in urging Turati towards the creation of a socialist party in Italy, on the German model, but at the last minute decided not to participate in the founding congress of the PSI at Genoa in 1892, because of his reservations about its ideological clarity.

main theoretical organ of the SPD and drafted the official programme of the party at the Erfurt Congress. Mehring was a prominent contributor to *Die Neue Zeit*, Labriola to its French counterpart *Le Devenir Social*. All four men personally corresponded with Engels, who was a formative influence on them. The main direction of their work can be seen, in fact, as a continuation of Engels's own final period. In other words, they were concerned in different ways to *systematize* historical materialism as a comprehensive theory of man and nature, capable of replacing rival bourgeois disciplines and providing the workers' movement with a broad and coherent vision of the world that could be easily grasped by its militants. This task involved them, as it had done for Engels, in a two-fold commitment: to produce general philosophical statements of Marxism as a conception of history, and to extend it into domains that had not been directly touched by Marx. The similarity of the titles of some of their main expositions indicates their common preoccupations: *On Historical Materialism* (Mehring), *Essays on the Materialist Conception of History* (Labriola), *The Development of the Monist Conception of History* (Plekhanov), *The Materialist Conception of History* (Kautsky).[5] At the same time, Mehring and Plekhanov wrote essays on literature and art (*The Lessing Legend* and *Art and Social Life*), while Kautsky turned to a study of religion (*The Origins of Christianity*) – all themes which the later Engels had briefly probed.[6] The general sense of these works was that of a completion, more than a development, of Marx's heritage. The start of scholarly publication of Marx's manuscripts and biographical study of his life, with the intention of recovering and displaying them in full to the socialist movement for the first time, also belongs to this generation. Engels had published the Second and Third Volumes of *Capital*; Kautsky then edited the *Theories of Surplus-Value*; Mehring subsequently collaborated in the publication of the *Marx-Engels Correspondence*; and at the end of his life he produced the first major biography of Marx.[7] Systematization and recapitulation of an in-

---

[5] Mehring's essay was published in 1893, Plekhanov's in 1895, Labriola's in 1896. Kautsky's treatise, on a far larger scale, was published much later, in 1927.

[6] These texts were written respectively in 1893 (Mehring), 1908 (Kautsky) and 1912–13 (Plekhanov).

[7] *Capital* Vol. II appeared in 1885, and Vol. III in 1896; *Theories of Surplus Value* from 1905–10; *Correspondence* in 1913; Mehring's *Karl Marx* in 1918.

heritance still very new and close behind them were the predominant aims of these successors.

Meanwhile, however, the whole international climate of world capitalism was altering. In the last years of the nineteenth century, there was a sharp economic upswing in the major industrial countries, as monopolization took grip at home and imperialist expansion accelerated abroad, inaugurating a tense era of impetuous technological innovation, rising rates of profit, increasing accumulation of capital, and escalating military rivalry between the great powers. These objective conditions were very different from the comparatively tranquil phase of capitalist development during the long recession from 1874 to 1894, after the defeat of the Commune and before the first outbreak of inter-imperialist conflicts in the Anglo-Boer and Spanish-American Wars (soon followed by the Russo-Japanese War). The immediate heirs of Marx and Engels had been formed in a period of relative lull. The next generation of Marxists came of age in a much more turbulent environment, as European capitalism began to scud towards the tempest of the First World War. The theoreticians of this levy were much more numerous than their predecessors; and they confirmed still more dramatically a shift that had already started to be visible in the previous period – the transference of the whole geographical axis of Marxist culture towards Eastern and Central Europe. The dominant figures of the new generation came without exception from regions east of Berlin. Lenin was the son of a civil servant from Astrakhan, Luxemburg the daughter of a timber-merchant from Galicia, Trotsky the son of a farmer from the Ukraine, Hilferding of an insurance functionary and Bauer of a textile manufacturer in Austria. All of these wrote major works before the First World War. Bukharin, the son of a teacher in Moscow, and Preobrazhensky, whose father was a priest from Orel, made their mark after it, but can be considered as later products of the same formation. The dating and distribution of the development of Marxist theory up to this point can thus be tabulated as follows:

Marx	1818–1883	Trier (Rhineland)
Engels	1820–1895	Barmen (Westphalia)

Labriola	1843–1904	Cassino (Campania)
Mehring	1846–1919	Schlawe (Pomerania)
Kautsky	1854–1938	Prague (Bohemia)
Plekhanov	1856–1918	Tambov (Central Russia)

Lenin	1870–1923	Simbirsk (Volga)
Luxemburg	1871–1919	Zamosc (Galicia)
Hilferding	1877–1941	Vienna
Trotsky	1879–1940	Kherson (Ukraine)
Bauer	1881–1938	Vienna
Preobrazhensky	1886–1937	Orel (Central Russia)
Bukharin	1888–1938	Moscow

Virtually all the younger generation of theorists were to play a commanding part in the leadership of their respective national parties – a role far more central and active than that of their predecessors. Lenin, of course, was the creator of the Bolshevik Party in Russia. Luxemburg was the guiding intellect of the Social-Democratic Party in Poland, and later the most authoritative founder of the Communist Party of Germany. Trotsky was a central figure in the factional disputes of Russian Social-Democracy, and Bukharin a rising lieutenant of Lenin, before the First World War. Bauer headed the secretariat of the parliamentary group of the Austrian Social-Democratic Party, while Hilferding became a prominent Reichstag deputy of the German Social-Democratic Party. A common feature of this whole group was the extraordinary precocity of their development: every single one of the figures just mentioned had written a basic theoretical work by the end of their twenties.

What were the new departures which their writing represented? Determined by the quickening of the whole historical tempo from the turn of the century onwards, their concerns lay essentially in two novel directions. Firstly, the manifest transformations of the capitalist mode of production that had generated monopolization and imperialism demanded sustained economic analysis and explanation. Marx's work was now, moreover, coming under professional criticism from academic economists for the first time.[8] *Capital* could no longer be simply rested on: it had to be developed. The first major attempt in this direction was actually undertaken by Kautsky, with his *Agrarian Question* in 1899, a sweeping categorial exploration of the changes in European and American agriculture which suggested that he was now the member of the older generation most sensitive to the needs of the contemporary situation, and sealed his authority among younger Marxists.[9] Later in the same year, Lenin published *The Development of Capitalism in Russia* – a massive study of a rural economy, whose formal inspiration was very close to that of the *Agrarian Question*, but whose specific objective was in some ways bolder and more novel. For this work was, in effect, the first serious application of the general theory of the capitalist mode of production set out in *Capital* to a concrete social formation, combining a number of modes of production in an articulated historical totality. Lenin's investigation of the Tsarist countryside thus represented a critical advance for historical materialism as a whole: he was twenty-nine when he completed it. Six years later, Hilferding – who had won his spurs in 1904 with an effective reply to Böhm-Bawerk's marginalist critique of Marx – finished his path-breaking study of *Finance Capital*, at the age of twenty-eight. Published in 1910, Hilferding's work went beyond either a 'sectoral' or a 'national' application of *Capital*, such as had been achieved by Kautsky and Lenin, to present a full-scale 'up-dating' of it, to take account of the global changes in the capitalist mode of production as such, in the new epoch of trusts, tariffs and trade wars. Centring his analysis on the growing ascendancy of banks, the accelerating thrust of monopolization, and the increasing use of state machinery for the aggressive expansion of capital, Hilferding stressed the mounting international tension and anarchy that was the concomitant of the tightening organization and

---

[8] The first serious neo-classical critique of Marx was Böhm-Bawerk's *Zum Abschluss des Marxschen Systems* (1896). Böhm-Bawerk was three times Finance Minister in the Austrian Empire, and held the chair of Political Economy at Vienna University from 1904 to 1914.

[9] Debate on agrarian problems within the SPD was in large measure originally set off by Max Weber's study of the conditions of agricultural labourers in East Germany published by the liberal *Verein für Sozialpolitik* in 1892. See Giuliano Procacci's excellent introduction to the recent Italian re-edition of Kautsky's work: *La Questione Agraria*, Milan 1971, pp. L–LII, LVIII.

centralization of each national capitalism. Meanwhile, in 1907 (after the completion of *Finance Capital* but before its publication), Bauer had published an equally large volume on *The Nationalities Question and Social Democracy*, when he was twenty-six. In this, he tackled a crucial political and theoretical problem that had scarcely been touched by Marx and Engels, and that was now looming larger than ever before the socialist movement: in this virtually new field, he developed an ambitious synthesis to explain the origin and composition of nations, concluding with an analysis of the contemporary surge of imperialist annexationism outside Europe. Imperialism itself next became the object of a major theoretical treatment in its own right, in Luxemburg's *Accumulation of Capital*, published on the very eve of the First World War in 1913. Luxemburg's insistence on the indispensable role of the non-capitalist hinterlands of capitalism in realizing surplus-value, and therefore of the structural necessity of military-imperial expansion by the metropolitan powers in the Balkans, Asia and Africa, marked her work – despite its analytical errors – as the most radical and original effort to rethink and develop the categorial system of *Capital* on a world scale, in the light of the new epoch. It was promptly criticized in *Die Neue Zeit* by Bauer, who had from 1904 onwards also been working on the problem of Marx's schemas for the expanded reproduction of capital. Finally, after the War itself had broken out, Bukharin presented his own account of the march of international capitalism in *Imperialism and the World Economy*, written in 1915;[10] while in the following year Lenin published his famous short study *Imperialism – The Highest Stage of Capitalism*, which both provided a descriptive summary of the common economic conclusions of the preceding debate, and for the first time framed them within a coherent political analysis of imperialist bellicism and colonial exploitation, derived from the general law of uneven development of the capitalist mode of production.

The first decade and a half of the century thus saw a great florescence of Marxist economic thought in Germany, Austria and Russia. Every major theorist of the time took for granted the vital importance of

[10] Bukharin later also published his own extended critique of Luxemburg's theory, in 1924; this text has recently been translated into English in K. Tarbuck (ed.), *Imperialism and the Accumulation of Capital*, London 1971.

deciphering the fundamental laws of motion of capitalism in its new stage of historical development. At the same time, however, there was also a meteoric emergence of a Marxist *political* theory for the first time. Whereas the economic studies of the period could build directly on the imposing foundations of *Capital*, neither Marx nor Engels had bequeathed any comparable corpus of concepts for the political strategy and tactics of the proletarian revolution. Their objective situation, as we have seen, precluded this. The rapid growth of working-class parties in Central Europe and the stormy rise of popular rebellions against the ancien régimes of Eastern Europe now created the conditions for a new type of theory, based directly on mass struggles of the proletariat and integrated naturally into party organizations. The Russian Revolution of 1905, closely watched throughout Germany and Austria, produced the first *strategic* political analysis of a scientific type in the history of Marxism: Trotsky's *Results and Prospects*. Grounded in a remarkable insight into the structure of the state system of world imperialism, this short work laid down with brilliant accuracy the future character and course of the socialist revolution in Russia. Written by Trotsky at the age of twenty-seven, it was not followed by any further contribution of importance from him before the First World War, given his isolation from the Bolshevik Party after 1907. The *systematic* construction of a Marxist political theory of class struggle, at the organizational and tactical level, was the work of Lenin. The scale of his accomplishment on this plane transformed the whole architecture of historical materialism, permanently. Before Lenin, the political domain proper was virtually unexplored within Marxist theory. In the space of some twenty years, he created the concepts and methods necessary for the conduct of a successful proletarian struggle for power in Russia, led by a skilled and devoted workers' party. The specific ways of combining propaganda and agitation, leading strikes and demonstrations, forging class alliances, cementing party organization, handling national self-determination, interpreting internal and international conjunctures, situating types of deviation, using parliamentary work, preparing insurrectionary assault – all these innovations, often seen as simply 'practical' measures, in fact also represented decisive *intellectual* advances into hitherto uncharted terrain. *What is to be Done?*, *One Step Forward Two Steps Back*, *Two Tactics of*

Social-Democracy, The Lessons of the Moscow Uprising, The Agrarian Programme of Russian Social-Democracy, The Right of Nations to Self-Determination – all these, and a hundred other 'occasional' articles or essays before the First World War, inaugurated a Marxist science of politics, henceforward capable of dealing with a vast range of problems which had previously lain outside any rigorous theoretical jurisdiction. The power of Lenin's work in these years was, of course, imparted to it by the immense revolutionary energies of the Russian masses under the twilight of Tsarism. Only their elemental spontaneous practice, pressing ever closer towards the overthrow of Russian Absolutism, rendered possible the great enlargement of Marxist theory achieved by Lenin.

Necessarily, too, it was once again these real material conditions of an intellectual discovery which determined its objective boundaries. There is no space here to discuss the limitations and oversights of Lenin's work: it can merely be said that these were all basically related to the particular backwardness of the Russian social formation, and the State which governed it, and which set the Tsarist Empire off from the rest of pre-war Europe. Lenin, far more deeply rooted in a national workers' movement than Marx had ever been, was not directly concerned with the necessarily distinct framework of struggle elsewhere in the continent, which was to make the road to revolution qualitatively more difficult than in Russia itself. Thus in Germany, industrially much more advanced, universal male suffrage and civic liberties had created a quite distinct state structure from the Romanov autocracy, and hence a political battle-field that never closely resembled that of Russia. There, the temper of the organized working class was notably less revolutionary, while at the same time its culture was considerably more developed, together with the institutional framework of the whole society. Luxemburg, the one Marxist thinker in Imperial Germany to produce an original body of political theory, suggestively reflected this contradiction in her own work – although it was always also partially informed by her experience of the much more insurgent Polish underground movement of the time. Luxemburg's political writings never attained the coherence or depth of those of Lenin, or the foresight of those of Trotsky. The soil of the German movement did not permit a comparable growth. But Luxemburg's passionate interventions within the SPD against its growing slide towards reformism (whose extent Lenin in exile notably failed to perceive) nevertheless contained elements of a critique of capitalist democracy, a defence of proletarian spontaneity, and a conception of socialist liberty that were in advance of Lenin's awareness of these issues, in her more complex environment. *Social Reform or Revolution*, the trenchant polemic with which she replied to Bernstein's evolutionism at the age of twenty-eight, launched her on her distinctive course: successive theorizations of the general strike as the archetypal aggressive weapon of the self-emancipation of the working class followed, reaching their conclusion in a fateful debate with Kautsky in 1909–10, in which the basic dividing-lines of future working-class politics were finally drawn.

For the First World War was to part the ranks of Marxist theory in Europe as radically as it split the working-class movement itself. The whole development of Marxism in the last decades before the War had realized a much closer unity of theory and practice than in the pre-ceding period, because of the ascent of the organized socialist parties of the time. The integration of the leading Marxist theorists into the practice of their national parties did not, however, provincialize or segregate them from each other. On the contrary, international debate and polemic were second nature to them: if none achieved the olympian universalism of Marx or Engels, this was a necessary consequence of their more concrete racination in the particular situation and life of their countries – mediated, in the case of the Russians and the Poles, by long spells of exile abroad, recalling those of the founders of historical materialism.[11] Within the new conditions of the epoch, they neverthe-less formed a relatively homogeneous medium of discussion and communication, in which the leading writers of the main detachments of the Second International in the Eastern and Central European countries, where Marxism was now concentrated as a living theory, knew of each other's work at first or second hand, and criticism respected no

[11] Some idea of the Russian emigration is suggested by the countries in which Lenin, Trotsky and Bukharin lived or travelled before 1917: They included Germany, England, France, Belgium, Switzerland and Austria (Lenin and Trotsky); Italy and Poland (Lenin); Rumania, Serbia, Bulgaria, Spain (Trotsky); USA (Trotsky and Bukharin); Denmark, Norway and Sweden (Bukharin).

frontiers. Thus when War broke out in 1914, the scission over it ran through rather than between the various national contingents of Marxist theorists who had dominated the pre-war scene. Of the older generation, Kautsky and Plekhanov clamorously opted for social chauvinism and support for their respective (opposing) imperialist fatherlands; Mehring, on the other hand, steadfastly refused to have any truck with the capitulation of the SPD in Germany. Among the younger generation, Lenin, Trotsky, Luxemburg and Bukharin flung themselves into all-out resistance to the War and denunciation of the betrayal of the contending social-democratic organizations which had ranged themselves behind their class oppressors in the long-predicted holocaust of capitalism. Hilferding, who had initially opposed the War in the Reichstag, soon allowed himself to be drafted into the Austrian Army; Bauer promptly rallied for service against Russia on the Eastern Front, where he was quickly captured. The unity and reality of the Second International, cherished by Engels, was destroyed in a week.

The continental consequences of August 1914 are well known. In Russia, a spontaneous rising of hungry and war-weary masses in Petrograd toppled Tsarism in February 1917. Within eight months, the Bolshevik Party under Lenin's leadership was ready to seize power. In October, Trotsky marshalled it in Petrograd for the Socialist revolution he had foreseen twelve years earlier. The swift victory of 1917 was soon followed by imperialist blockade, intervention and the civil war of 1918–21. The epic course of the Russian Revolution in these years found its theoretical compass in the writings of Lenin, in whom political thought and action now fused into a quickened unity without precedent or sequel. From the *April Theses* through *State and Revolution* and *Marxism and Insurrection* to *Left-Wing Communism* and *The Tax in Kind*, Lenin's works of these years established new norms within historical materialism – the 'concrete analysis of a concrete situation' which he called the 'living soul of Marxism' acquiring such a dynamic force in them that the term Leninism as such came into use shortly afterwards. In this heroic period of the pro-letarian revolution in Russia, of course, the rapid development of Marxist theory was by no means confined to Lenin's own work. Trotsky wrote fundamental texts on the art of war (*How the Revolution Armed Itself*) and the destiny of literature (*Literature and Revolution*).

Bukharin attempted to summarize historical materialism as a systematic sociology in a widely discussed treatise (*Theory of Historical Materialism*).[12] Shortly afterwards, Preobrazhensky, with whom he had collaborated on the popular Bolshevik manual *The ABC of Communism*, started to publish the most original and radical economic study of the tasks before the Soviet State in the transition towards socialism – a field hitherto naturally untrespassed by Marxist theory; the first parts of the *New Economics* appeared in 1924. At the same time, the international centre of gravity of the historical scholarship devoted to the discovery and editing of Marx's unpublished writings shifted to Russia. Ryazanov, who already before the First World War had established his reputation for archival research on Marx, now took charge of the first complete and scientific edition of the works of Marx and Engels, the bulk of whose manuscripts were transferred to Moscow and deposited in the Marx-Engels Institute of which he had become the director.[13] All these men held, of course, prominent positions in the practical struggle for the triumph of the revolution in Russia, and in the construction of the nascent Soviet state. During the Civil War, Lenin was Chairman of the Council of People's Commissars, Trotsky was Commissar for War, Bukharin was editor of the Party newspaper, Preobrazhensky was effectively the first head of the Party secretariat, Ryazanov was organizer of the trade-unions. The pleiad of this generation, in their prime when the Civil War was fought to a successful conclusion, appeared to assure the future of Marxist culture in the new workers' fortress of the USSR.

In the rest of Europe, however, the great revolutionary wave which broke out in 1918 at the end of the War, and lasted until 1920, was defeated. Capital proved decisively stronger everywhere outside Russia. The international counter-revolutionary encirclement of the Soviet State in the years 1918–21 did not succeed in overthrowing it,

[12] Bukharin's manual of sociology was published in 1921; Trotsky's study on literature in 1924.

[13] David Ryazanov (real name Golden'dakh) was born in 1870. It was a dispute over his admission to the Second Congress of the RSDLP which initially split Martov from Lenin, just prior to their conflict over the rules of party organization. After the 1905 Revolution Ryazanov had published frequent articles in *Die Neue Zeit*, and had worked on the editing of the Marx-Engels correspondence.

although the Civil War inflicted enormous damage on the Russian working class. But it did seal the Russian Revolution tightly off from the rest of Europe during the three years of most acute social crisis for the imperialist order in the whole continent, and so allowed the proletarian risings outside the Soviet Union to be successfully checked. The first and most fundamental threat to the much more entrenched capitalist states of the continent was the great series of mass revolts in Germany in 1918–19. Luxemburg, observing the course of the Russian Revolution from prison, characteristically discerned certain of the dangers of the dictatorship installed during the Civil War more clearly than any Bolshevik leader of the time, while at the same time also often revealing the limits of her own grasp of those issues (nationality, peasantry) whose significance was less obvious in the highly industrialized zones of Europe.[14] Released from imprisonment with the collapse of the Second Reich, Luxemburg immediately threw herself into the task of organizing the revolutionary left in Germany; as the most authoritative figure in the formation of the KPD a month later, she wrote the programme of the party and delivered the political report at its founding Conference. Two weeks later, she was assassinated when a confused, semi-spontaneous rising started amongst the famished Berlin crowds was put down by the Freikorps at the behest of a Social-Democratic government. The repression of the January insurrection in Berlin was soon followed by the military reconquest of Munich by the Reichswehr, after local socialist and communist groups had created an ephemeral Bavarian Soviet Republic there in April. The German Revolution born of the workers' and soldiers' councils of November 1918 had been decisively defeated by 1920.

Meanwhile, in the Austro-Hungarian Empire, a comparable pattern of events had unfolded. In the more backward rural state of Hungary, Entente demands had led to the voluntary abdication of the bourgeois government set up after the Armistice, and the brief creation of a Soviet Republic under joint Social-Democratic and Communist leadership: six months later, Rumanian troops had suppressed the Hungarian Commune and restored a white régime. In Austria, the objective weight of the industrial working class was much greater than

[14] Her essay, *The Russian Revolution*, written in 1918, was first published by Paul Levi in 1922.

in Hungary (as it had been in Prussia compared to Bavaria), but the Social-Democratic Party – unchallenged in its command of the loyalties of the proletariat – opted against a socialist revolution, entering instead into a bourgeois coalition government, and gradually dismantling the workers' and soldiers' councils from above, on the pretext of avoiding Entente intervention. By 1920, it had abandoned the government, but capitalist restabilization was by then assured. Bauer, who soon became the dominant figure within the ÖSPD, served as Foreign Minister of the Republic in 1919, and subsequently wrote the major theoretical defence of the party's record after the war, a volume miscalled *The Austrian Revolution*, in 1924. His former colleague Hilferding, meanwhile, was twice to be Minister of Finance in the Weimar Republic. The unity of theory and practice characteristic of this generation was sustained even in the reformist ranks of Austro-Marxism.[15] Farther south, the last major proletarian upsurge of the post-war triennium occurred in Italy. The homeland of Labriola had always had a much smaller socialist party than Germany or Austro-Hungary, but a more militant one: it had resisted social patriotism and flaunted a verbal maximalism during the War. But the general strike and tumultuous wave of factory occupations which gripped Turin in 1920 nevertheless found it, too, completely unprepared for an aggressive revolutionary strategy; the rapid counter-measures of the Liberal government and the employers eventually paralyzed the movement, in the absence of any clear political leadership. The tide of popular insurgency ebbed away, leaving the armed squads of counter-revolution to prepare the advent of fascism in Italy.

The fateful setbacks in Germany, Austria, Hungary and Italy – the classical zone of influence of pre-war Marxism, together with Russia – occurred before the Bolshevik Revolution was itself sufficiently dis-engaged from imperialist intervention to be able to exercise a direct organizational or theoretical influence on the course of the class struggle in these countries. The Third International was technically founded in 1919, when Moscow was still a city beleaguered by white

[15] Two other prominent economists, one an ex-Marxist and the other a critic of Marxism, held governmental posts in this epoch in East-Central Europe. In the Ukraine, Tugan-Baranovsky was Minister of Finance in the counter-revolutionary Rada of 1917–18; while in Austria, Schumpeter held the same position in 1919.

armies: its real creation dates from its Second Congress in July 1920. By then it was too late to have any impact on the pivotal battles of the post-war conjuncture. The advance of the Red Army into Poland, which briefly seemed to promise the possibility of a material link with the revolutionary forces in Central Europe, was thrown back in the same month; and within a few weeks, the Turinese occupations had collapsed, while Lenin was appealing by telegraph to the PSI for a national action in Italy. These defeats were not, of course, primarily due to subjective mistakes or failures: the latter were a sign of the objectively superior strength of capitalism in Central and Western Europe, where its historical ascendancy over the working class had survived the war. It was not until after these battles had been fought and lost, that the Third International became solidly implanted in the major continental countries outside the USSR. Once the blockade of the Soviet State was finally broken, of course, the enormous contrast between the debacle of the social-democratic apparatuses and defeat of the spontaneous risings in Central and Southern Europe on the one hand, and the success of the Bolshevik Party in Russia on the other, ensured the relatively rapid formation of a centralized revolutionary international based on principles drafted by Lenin and Trotsky. In 1921, Lenin composed his fundamental theoretical 'message' to the new Communist Parties that had now been founded virtually everywhere in the advanced capitalist world: *Leftwing Communism – An Infantile Disorder*. In this he synthesized the historical lessons of Bolshevik experience in Russia for socialists abroad, and started to address himself for the first time to the problems of Marxist strategy in more advanced environments than that of the Tsarist Empire, in which bourgeois parliamentarism was far stronger and working-class reformism much deeper than he had realized before the First World War. Systematic translation now, too, for the first time revealed Lenin's work as an organized theoretical system to militants throughout Europe, coming as a sudden political illumination to thousands of them. The conditions for an international diffusion and fertilization of Marxist theory, on a wholly new scale, now seemed to be present, and the Comintern the guarantee of its material linkage with the daily struggles of the masses.

In fact, this prospect was rapidly annulled. The savage blows inflicted by imperialism on the Russian Revolution itself had decimated the Soviet working class, even amidst its military victory over the white forces in the Civil War. After 1920, no immediate relief could be expected from the more developed countries of Europe. The USSR was condemned to isolation, its industry ruined, its proletariat weakened, its agriculture laid waste, its peasantry disaffected. Capitalist restabilization had been accomplished in Central Europe while revolutionary Russia was cut off from it. No sooner had encirclement been broken and contact re-established with the rest of the continent, than the Soviet state – caught in the vice of Russian backwardness, without political aid from abroad – started to become endangered at home. The hardening usurpation of power by the Party apparatus, the tightening subordination of the working class, the mounting tide of official chauvinism, belatedly became evident to Lenin himself, after he had fallen mortally ill in 1922. His last writings – from his article on *Rabkrin* to his *Testament*[16] – can be seen as a desperate theoretical attempt to find the forms to permit a revival of a genuine political practice of the masses, which could explode the bureaucratism of the new Soviet State, and restore the lost unity and democracy of October.

In early 1924, Lenin died. Within three years, Stalin's victory inside the CPSU sealed the fate of socialism, and Marxism, within the USSR for decades to come. Stalin's political apparatus actively suppressed revolutionary mass practices in Russia itself, and increasingly discouraged or sabotaged them outside the Soviet Union. The consolidation of a bureaucratically privileged stratum above the working class was secured by a police regime of ever intensifying ferocity. In these conditions, the revolutionary unity of theory and practice that had made possible classical Bolshevism was ineluctably destroyed. The masses below were interdicted, their autonomy and spontaneity extinguished by the bureaucratic caste that had confiscated power in the country. The party above was gradually purged of the last companions of Lenin. All serious theoretical work ceased in the Soviet Union after collectivization. Trotsky was driven into exile in 1929, and assassinated in 1940; Ryazanov was stripped of his positions in 1931 and died in a labour camp in 1939; Bukharin was silenced in 1929

---

[16] Lenin, *Collected Works*, Vol. 33, pp. 481–502; Vol. 36, pp. 593–7.

and shot in 1938; Preobrazhensky was broken by 1930 and perished in jail in 1938. Marxism was largely reduced to a memento in Russia, as Stalin's rule reached its apogee. The most advanced country in the world in the development of historical materialism, which had outdone all Europe by the variety and vigour of its theorists, was turned within a decade into a semi-literate backwater, formidable only by the weight of its censorship and the crudity of its propaganda.

Meanwhile outside the USSR, while Stalinism fell like a hood over Soviet culture, the political physiognomy of European capitalism was becoming increasingly violent and convulsed. The working class had everywhere suffered defeat in the great post-war revolutionary crisis: but it remained a powerful threat to the bourgeoisies throughout Central and Southern Europe. The creation of the Third International and the growth of disciplined Communist parties, bearing the standard of Leninism, inspired fear in every ruling class of the original epicentres of 1918–20. Moreover, the economic recovery of imperialism that had succeeded and secured the political restabilization of the Versailles order proved short-lived. In 1929, the greatest crash in the history of capitalism overwhelmed the continent, spreading mass unemployment and intensifying class struggle. Social counter-revolution now mobilized in its most brutal and violent forms, abolishing parliamentary democracy in country after country, to eliminate all autonomous organizations of the working class. The terrorist dictatorships of fascism were the historical solution of capital to the dangers of labour in this region: they were designed to suppress every trace of proletarian resistance and independence, in an international conjuncture of escalating inter-imperialist antagonisms. Italy was the first country to experience the full force of fascist repression: by 1926 Mussolini had ended all legal opposition within the country. Nazism seized power in Germany in 1933, after the Comintern had imposed a suicidal course on the KPD; the German labour movement was annihilated. A year later, clerical fascism unleashed an armed assault in Austria which destroyed the party and trade-union strongholds of the working class. In Hungary, a white dictatorship had already long been installed. To the South, a military putsch in Spain inaugurated three years of civil war which ended with the triumph of Spanish fascism, assisted by its neighbour in Portugal and its allies in Italy and Germany. The decade ended with the Nazi occupation and control of Czechoslovakia, and the fall of France.

In this catastrophic epoch, what was the fate of Marxist theory in the Central European zone which had played such an important role in the development of historical materialism before the First World War? Leninist political thought, as we have seen, was no sooner diffused outside Russia than it was sterilized by the Stalinization of the Third International, which progressively subordinated the policies of its constituent parties to the foreign policy objectives of the USSR. The social-democratic or centrist parties outside the Comintern naturally offered no space for the application or extension of Leninism either. Thus within the ambit of the mass working-class organizations of this zone, Marxist theory of substance in the inter-war period was largely confined to economic analysis, in a line that was a direct descendant of the great pre-war debates. In the Weimar Republic, an independent Institute of Social Research, endowed by a wealthy grain merchant, was created at Frankfurt in 1923 to promote Marxist studies within a quasi-academic framework (the Institute was formally attached to the University of Frankfurt).[17] Its first director was the legal historian Carl Grünberg, who had held a chair at the University of Vienna before the First World War. Born in Transylvania in 1861, Grünberg was a typical member of the older generation of Marxist scholars from Eastern Europe; he had founded and edited the first major journal of labour history in Europe, the *Archiv für die Geschichte des Sozialismus und der Arbeiterbewegung*, which he now transferred to Frankfurt. This distinguished representative of the Austro-Marxist tradition henceforward formed a bridge to a younger generation of socialist intellectuals in Germany. During the twenties, the Institute of Social Research over which he presided had both Communists and Social-Democrats on its staff, and maintained a regular liaison with the Marx-Engels Institute in Moscow, dispatching archival material to Ryazanov for the first scientific edition of the works of Marx and Engels. The inaugural volume of the *Marx-Engels Gesamtausgabe* (MEGA) was, in fact,

---

[17] For the origins of the Frankfurt Institute of Social Research, see the full and scholarly account in Martin Jay, *The Dialectical Imagination*, London 1973, pp. 4–12 ff.

published in Frankfurt in 1927 under the joint auspices of the two institutions.

During the same period, the Institute also sponsored the major single product of Marxist economic theory in the inter-war years, the work of Henryk Grossmann – another emigrant from the Eastern borderlands of the continent. Born in 1881 in Cracow, the son of a Galician mine-owner, Grossmann was the same age as Bauer and seven years older than Bukharin – in other words, one of the outstanding generation that had risen to such heights before 1914. Grossmann, however, had developed more slowly: originally a student under Böhm-Bawerk in Vienna, he had joined the Polish Communist Party after the First World War and occupied a chair of economics at Warsaw University. In 1925 political repression drove him from Poland to Germany, and in 1926–7 he delivered a series of lectures at the Frankfurt Institute which were later collected to form a long volume entitled *The Law of Accumulation and Collapse of the Capitalist System*.[18] Published in the very year of the Great Depression of 1929, Grossmann's work summarized the classical pre-war debates on the laws of motion of the capitalist mode of production in the twentieth century, and advanced the most ambitious and systematic attempt so far to deduce its objective collapse from the logic of Marx's schemas of reproduction. Its central theses, which appeared to be so timely, were promptly challenged by the younger economist Fritz Sternberg, a left social-democrat. Sternberg's own work *Imperialism* (1926), which had largely been a restatement of Luxemburg's perspective, extended by a novel analysis of the functions and fluctuations of the reserve army of labour in capitalism, had earlier been attacked by Grossmann. Both parties were in turn criticized by another Marxist of Polish origin, Natalie Moszkowska, in a short book on modern theories of crisis written after the Nazi seizure of power in Germany.[19] In the following year, Bauer published his last theoretical work, prophetically entitled *Between Two World Wars?*, in exile in Czechoslovakia.[20] In this

[18] *Die Akkumulations- und Zusammenbruchsgesetz des kapitalistischen Systems*, Leipzig 1929; reissued in Frankfurt 1971.
[19] *Zur Kritik moderner Krisentheorien*, Prague 1935. Moszkowska was born in Warsaw in 1886, and emigrated to Switzerland in 1908, where she lived in Zurich until her death in 1968.
[20] *Zwischen Zwei Weltkriegen?*, Bratislava 1936.

political and economic testament, the most gifted exponent of the Austro-Marxist school perfected a life-time of experimentation with Marx's reproduction schemes to construct the most sophisticated case for an underconsumptionist theory of capitalist crises yet presented, and recorded his final disillusionment with the gradualist reformism which he had so long practised as a party leader, calling for a re-unification of the social-democratic and communist movements in the struggle against fascism.

In 1938, Bauer died in Paris, shortly after the Munich pact had driven him from Bratislava. Within a few months, the Second World War had broken out, and the Nazi engulfment of Europe closed an epoch of Marxism in the continent. In 1941, Hilferding perished at the hands of the Gestapo in Paris. It was now only in the wings of the battle-field that the post-scripts to the tradition they had incarnated could be written. In 1943 in Switzerland, Moszkowska published her last and most radical work, *On the Dynamic of Late Capitalism*.[21] Meanwhile in the United States, the young American economist Paul Sweezy retraced and summarized the whole history of the Marxist debates on the laws of motion of capitalism, from Tugan-Baranovsky to Grossmann, himself endorsing Bauer's last solution of the problem of underconsumption, in a work of model clarity, *The Theory of Capitalist Development*.[22] However, Sweezy's book, written in the environment of the New Deal, implicitly renounced the assumption that crises of disproportionality or underconsumption were insurmountable within the capitalist mode of production, and accepted the potential efficacy of Keynesian counter-cyclical interventions by the State to assure the internal stability of imperialism. The ultimate disintegration of capitalism was for the first time entrusted to a purely external determinant – the superior economic performance of the Soviet Union and the countries which could be expected to follow its path at the end of the War, whose 'persuasion effect' would eventually render possible a peaceful transition to socialism in the United States itself.[23] With this conception, *The Theory of Capitalist Development* marked the end of an intellectual age.

[21] *Zur Dynamik des Spätkapitalismus*, Zurich 1943.
[22] Sweezy was thirty-two when it was published in 1942.
[23] *The Theory of Capitalist Development*, New York 1968 re-edition, pp. 348–62.

2

The Advent of
Western Marxism

The tide of the Second World War duly turned at the Volga. The victories of the Red Army over the Wehrmacht in 1942–3 ensured the liberation of Europe from Nazi domination. By 1945, fascism had been defeated everywhere, except in its Iberian region. The USSR, enormously strengthened in international power and prestige, was master of the fate of Eastern Europe, with the exception of the southernmost Balkans. Communist régimes were soon installed in Prussia, Czechoslovakia, Poland, Hungary, Rumania, Bulgaria, Yugoslavia and Albania; the local capitalist classes were expropriated; Soviet-style industrialization was launched. An integrated 'socialist camp' now covered half the continent. The other half was rescued for capitalism by the American and British armies. In France and Italy, however, their leading role in the Resistance converted the national Communist Parties for the first time into the majority organizations of the working class. In Western Germany, on the other hand, the absence of a comparable resistance experience and the division of the country permitted a successful elimination of the pre-war Communist tradition in the proletariat by the restored bourgeois State, under the protection of Anglo-American occupation. The next twenty years exhibited an economic and political pattern diametrically contrasted with that of the inter-war period. There were no reversions to military or police dictatorships in the major West European countries. Parliamentary democracy, based on fully universal suffrage, for the first time in the history of capitalism became stable and normal throughout the advanced industrial world. Nor was there any repetition of the catastrophic slumps of the twenties and thirties. On the contrary, world capitalism enjoyed a long boom of unprecedented dynamism, the most rapid and prosperous phase of expansion in its history. Meanwhile, the repressive bureaucratic regimes exercising tutelage over the proletariat in the Soviet Union and Eastern Europe underwent successive crises and adjustments after the death of Stalin, but no fundamental modification of their structure. Terror was abandoned as a systematic weapon of the State, but armed coercion continued to subdue popular revolts in this zone. Economic growth was swift, from its comparatively low starting-points, but represented no political challenge to the stability of the capitalist bloc.

It was in this altered universe that revolutionary theory completed the mutation which produced what can today retrospectively be called 'Western Marxism'. For the body of work composed by the authors with whom we shall now be concerned, in effect constituted an entirely new intellectual configuration within the development of historical materialism. In their hands, Marxism became a type of theory in certain critical respects quite distinct from anything that had preceded it. In particular, the characteristic themes and concerns of the whole ensemble of theorists who came to political maturity before the First World War were drastically displaced, in a shift that was at once generational and geographical.

The history of this displacement was a long and complex one, its inception starting in the inter-war period itself, and overlapping with the declension of an earlier tradition. The clearest way of approaching this problem may be via a simple initial tabulation of the dates and distribution of the theorists now under discussion:

Lukács	1885–1971	Budapest
Korsch	1886–1961	Todstedt (West Saxony)
Gramsci	1891–1937	Ales (Sardinia)
Benjamin	1892–1940	Berlin
Horkheimer	1895–1973	Stuttgart (Swabia)
Della Volpe	1897–1968	Imola (Romagna)
Marcuse	1898	Berlin
Lefebvre	1901	Hagetmau (Gascony)
Adorno	1903–1969	Frankfurt

Sartre	1905	Paris
Goldmann	1913–1970	Bucharest
Althusser	1918	Birmandreis (Algeria)
Colletti	1924	Rome

The social origins of these thinkers were not dissimilar to those of their predecessors.[1] Geographically, however, the pattern of this group marks a radical contrast with that of the Marxist intellectuals who came to prominence after Engels. As we have seen, virtually every important theorist of the two succeeding generations after the founders of historical materialism themselves, was from Eastern or East-Central Europe; even within the Germanic Empires, it was Vienna and Prague rather than Berlin that provided the major luminaries of the Second International. From the end of the First World War onwards, on the other hand, the position was reversed. With the central exception of Lukács, and his pupil Goldmann, every significant figure in the tradition indicated above was from farther West. Lukács himself was largely formed at Heidelberg, and always remained more German than Hungarian in culture; while Goldmann lived in France and Switzerland throughout his adult life. Of the two Germans who were born in Berlin, Benjamin was notably and self-consciously Gallic in cultural orientation; while Marcuse received his main training at Freiburg in Swabia.[2] Two generational divisions can be made within this tradition.[3]

[1] Lukács was the son of a banker; Benjamin of an art-dealer; Adorno of a wine-merchant; Horkheimer of a textile-manufacturer; Della Volpe of a landowner; Sartre of a naval officer; Korsch and Althusser of bank managers; Colletti of a bank clerk; Lefebvre of a bureaucrat; Goldmann of a lawyer. Gramsci, uniquely, was brought up in conditions of real poverty; his grandfather had been a police colonel, but his father's career as a minor civil servant was ruined when he was jailed for corruption, and the family suffered great hardship thereafter.

[2] South-West Germany seems to have played an important role as a distinct cultural zone in this tradition. Adorno and Horkheimer were native to it, Lukács and Marcuse were trained in it. Heidelberg and Freiburg had close philosophical links from the time of the Second Reich onwards. For Benjamin's Francophilia, see his remark as early as 1927: 'In Germany, I feel quite isolated in my efforts and interests among those of my generation, while in France there are certain forces . . . in which I see at work what occupies me too.' *Illuminations*, London 1970, p. 22.

[3] Any generational classification must be based on approximately twenty-year

The first group of intellectuals were those whose formative political experience was the First World War itself, or the influence of the Russian Revolution which occurred before it had ended. Biographically, Lukács was three years older than Bukharin, Korsch two years older. But what separated them from the pre-war generation of Marxists was that they came to revolutionary socialism much later; while Bukharin was already an active and tempered lieutenant of Lenin well before 1914, they were first radicalized by the Great War and the mass upheavals which followed it, emerging as Marxists only after 1918. Gramsci, on the other hand, was already a militant in the PSI on the eve of the First World War, but was still a young and immature one, whose inexperience led him to commit serious mistakes at its outset (when he came close to advocating Italian intervention in the holocaust, at a time when his party vigorously denounced it). Marcuse was drafted into the German Army before the age of twenty-one, briefly entering the USPD in 1917-18; Benjamin evaded military service but was swung left by the war. By contrast, the second generational 'set' within the tradition of Western Marxism was comprised of men who came to maturity well after the First World War, and who were politically formed by the advance of fascism and the Second World War. The first of these to discover historical materialism was Lefebvre, in many ways an unusual figure in this group, who joined the French Communist Party in 1928. Adorno, a decade younger than Marcuse or Benjamin, does not seem to have turned towards Marxism until after the Nazi seizure of power in 1933. Sartre and Althusser, although widely separated in age, appear to have been radicalized at the same time, by the impact of the Spanish Civil War, the French debacle of 1940, and imprisonment in Germany. Both completed their political evolution after 1945, in the first years of the Cold War: Althusser joined the PCF in 1948, while Sartre aligned himself with the inter-national Communist movement in 1950. Goldmann came under the spell of Lukács's work before and during the Second World War, encountering him in Switzerland after it in 1946. Della Volpe forms a

---

intervals, obviously: the problem is to know where to locate the relevant historical breaks within the biological continuum of lives in any epoch. There is no room to explore the subject adequately here. The critical lines of division in this case, however, are fairly clearly drawn by the successive political upheavals of the time.

chronological exception that nevertheless confirms the generational-political pattern: in age-group a member of the first generation, he remained completely untouched by the First World War, was later compromised by Italian fascism, and only belatedly moved in the direction of Marxism in 1944–5 at the end of the Second World War, when he was in his late forties. Finally, a single borderline case of a third generation is discernible: Colletti, who was too young to be deeply marked by the Second World War, and became a pupil of Della Volpe in the post-war period, joining the PCI in 1950.

Essentially, it will be seen, from the early twenties onwards European Marxism became increasingly concentrated in Germany, France and Italy – three countries which, either before or after the Second World War, combined a mass Communist Party commanding the allegiance of major sections of the working class, with a numerous and radical intelligentsia. The absence of one or other of these conditions blocked the emergence of a developed Marxist culture outside this zone. In Britain, a widespread radicalization occurred among intellectuals in the inter-war period, but the mass of the working class remained steadily loyal to social-democratic reformism. In Spain, the proletariat proved more revolutionary in temper than any other working class in the continent during the thirties, but there were very few intellectuals in the labour movement. Neither country produced any significant Marxist theory as such in this period.[4]

[4] The Spanish case, however, remains an important historical enigma. Why did Spain never produce a Labriola or a Gramsci – despite the extraordinary combativity of its proletariat and peasantry, more than equal to those of Italy, and a cultural heritage from the nineteenth century which, although certainly less than that of Italy, was far from negligible? A great deal of further research is needed into this complex problem. A solution of it would be central to any wider analysis of the conditions of emergence and development of historical materialism as a theory. Here it may merely be noted that – so far as the problem of relative cultural heritages is concerned – strikingly, while Croce was studying and advertising the work of Marx in Italy during the 1890s, the nearest analogous intellectual in Spain, Unamuno, was likewise converted to Marxism. Unamuno indeed, unlike Croce, actively participated in the organization of the Spanish Socialist Party in 1894–7. Yet whereas Croce's engagement with historical materialism was to have profound consequences for the development of Marxism in Italy, Unamuno's left no traces in Spain. The encyclopaedism of the Italian, so contrasted with the essayism of the Spaniard, was surely one of the reasons for the differential result of the two episodes. Unamuno was a far lesser thinker. More generally, his limitations were symptomatic of the much wider absence in Spain

The historical dates and geographical distribution of 'Western Marxism' provide the preliminary formal framework for situating it within the evolution of socialist thought as a whole. It remains to identify the specific substantive traits which define and demarcate it as an integrated tradition. The first and most fundamental of its characteristics has been the structural divorce of this Marxism from political practice. The organic unity of theory and practice realized in the classical generation of Marxists before the First World War, who performed an inseparably politico-intellectual function within their respective parties in Eastern and Central Europe, was to be increasingly severed in the half-century from 1918 to 1968, in Western Europe. The rupture between the two was not immediate or spontaneous, in the new generational and geographical context of Marxism after the First World War. It was slowly and progressively brought about by massive historical pressures, which only achieved the final breakage of the bond between theory and practice during the 1930s. By the epoch after the Second World War, however, the distance between them was so great that it seemed virtually consubstantial with the tradition itself. In fact, however, the first three important theoreticians of the post-1920 generation – the real originators of the whole pattern of Western Marxism – were all initially major political leaders within their own parties: Lukács, Korsch and Gramsci. Each, too, was a direct participant and organizer in the revolutionary mass upheavals of the time; the emergence of their theory cannot, indeed, be understood except against this political background.

Lukács was a Deputy People's Commissar for Education in the

---

of any major tradition of systematic philosophical thought – something that Spanish culture, for all the virtuosity of its literature, painting or music, had lacked from the Renaissance to the Enlightenment. It was perhaps the absence of this catalyst which prevented the emergence of any Marxist work of note in the Spanish labour movement of the twentieth century. This might also help to explain the curious failure of Marxism to develop a conventional constellation of theory in England, with its native tradition of empiricism (abruptly and sharply accentuated after 1900), while it produced a remarkable corpus of historiography. The importance of a philosophical element within the complex social synthesis necessary to generate a lively Marxism in any given national formation was, of course, classically emphasized by Engels. An awareness of this should temper critical assessment of the predominance of philosophy in Western Marxism elsewhere in Europe, surveyed later; it need not inhibit it.

Hungarian Soviet Republic in 1919, and fought with its revolutionary army on the Tisza front against the Entente attack on it. Exiled in Austria during the twenties, he was a leading member of the Hungarian Communist Party and after a decade of factional struggle within its organization, briefly became general secretary of the Party in 1928. Korsch was Communist Minister of Justice in the Thuringian government in 1923, charged with regional para-military preparations for the insurrection of the KPD in Central Germany during that year, which was preempted by the Reichswehr. He then became a prominent Reichstag deputy for the party; the editor of its theoretical journal; and one of the leaders of its left faction in 1925. Gramsci, of course, played a far more significant role than either of these two in the mass struggles of the immediate post-war epoch. The central organizer and theorist of the Turin factory councils and editor of *L'Ordine Nuovo* in 1919–20, he was one of the founding members of the PCI the following year, and gradually rose to become the dominant leader of the Party in 1924, when it was fighting a difficult defensive struggle against fascist consolidation in Italy. The fate of each of these three men symbolized the forces that were to split Marxist theory wide apart from any class practice in the subsequent years. Korsch was expelled from the KPD in 1926 for denying that capitalism had been stabilized, demanding renewed agitational emphasis on workers' councils, and criticizing Soviet foreign policy for accommodation with world capitalism. He then tried to maintain an independent political group for two years, and even after its dissolution remained active in Marxist intellectual and proletarian circles up to 1933, when the victory of Nazism drove him from Germany into exile and isolation in Scandinavia and the United States.[5] Lukács, on the other hand, drafted the official theses for the Hungarian Communist Party in 1928, which implicitly rejected the catastrophist perspectives just adopted at the Sixth Comintern Congress – the notorious 'Third Period' line with its violent attacks on reformist workers' organizations as 'social-fascist', and its nihilist denial of any distinction between bourgeois-democratic régimes and military-police dictatorships as instruments of capitalist rule.[6] Lukács's attempt to

[5] For this trajectory, see Hedda Korsch, 'Memories of Karl Korsch', *New Left Review*, No. 76, November–December 1972, pp. 42–4.
[6] See the key passages of the so-called Blum Theses (after Lukács's under-

sketch a differential typology of capitalist political systems in the new conjuncture, and his emphasis on the need for transitional democratic slogans in the struggle against Horthy's tyranny in Hungary, was violently denounced by the Comintern Secretariat, and he was threatened with summary ejection from the Party. To avoid expulsion, he published a recantation (without modifying his private views): but the price of his disavowal was a permanent renunciation of organizational responsibilities within his party or the International. From 1929 onwards, Lukács ceased to be a political militant, confining himself to literary criticism and philosophy in his intellectual work. After a brief period in Berlin, the Nazi seizure of power forced him too into exile – in the opposite direction, to the USSR, where he remained until the end of the Second World War.

Gramsci's destiny was darker. Arrested at Mussolini's orders in Rome in 1926, when Italian fascism finalized its complete dictatorship over the country, he spent nine terrible years in prison, in conditions which eventually killed him in 1937. Isolated by imprisonment from participation in the clandestine life of the PCI, he was saved from direct confrontation with the consequences of the Stalinization of the Comintern. Even so, his last political act before arrest was to write a sharp protest to Togliatti in Moscow against the latter's suppression of the Italian Party's letter to the Central Committee of the CPSU arguing for greater tolerance in its internal disputes, on the eve of the expulsion of the Left Opposition in Russia; while from within prison he later categorically opposed the 'third period' line from 1930 onwards, maintaining positions not unlike those of Lukács in 1928, which stressed the importance of intermediate democratic demands under fascism, and the vital need to win the alliance of the peasantry to overthrow it.[7] The climate of the time within the Third International was such that his brother, to whom he entrusted his views for transmission to the party centre outside Italy, remained silent in order to save him from the risk of expulsion. The two great tragedies which in such different ways overtook the European working-class movement

---

ground pseudonym), in Georg Lukács, *Political Writings 1919–1929*, London NLB 1972, pp. 240–51.

[7] See Giuseppe Fiori, *Antonio Gramsci*, London NLB 1970, pp. 249–58.

in the inter-war period, Fascism and Stalinism, thus combined to scatter and destroy the potential bearers of an indigenous Marxist theory united to the mass practice of the Western proletariat. Gramsci's solitude and death in Italy, Korsch's and Lukács's isolation and exile in the USA and USSR, marked the end of the phase in which Western Marxism was still at home among the masses. Henceforward, it was to speak its own enciphered language, at an increasingly remote distance from the class whose fortunes it formally sought to serve or articulate.

The deep change that was now to occur found its first expression in Germany. Its locus was the Institute for Social Research at Frankfurt, whose early origins and development have already been seen. Although its conception as an academic centre for Marxist research within a capitalist state was a new departure in the history of socialism – implying an institutional separation from politics that Luxemburg, for example, would never have accepted before the war – it had been devoted throughout the twenties to traditional problems of the workers' movement, combining solid empirical work with serious theoretical analysis. Its director specifically warned of the dangers of its becoming a school for 'mandarins' in his inaugural address, and its staff included active members of the proletarian parties of the Weimar Republic, especially the KPD.[8] The Institute's journal published work by Korsch and Lukács, side by side with essays by Grossmann or Ryazanov. It thus formed the nodal point of juncture at which 'Western' and 'Eastern' currents met within Marxism in the twenties. Its trajectory was consequently to be of critical importance for the evolution of Marxist theory as a whole, in inter-war Europe. In 1929 Grünberg, the Austro-Marxist historian who had directed it since its foundation, retired. In 1930, Horkheimer became the new director of the Institute: a year after Lukács had been silenced, in the year that Gramsci was censored for his own safety even in prison. A philosopher where Grünberg had been a historian, Horkheimer in his inaugural address set the tone for a major reorientation of the Institute's work, away from a concern with historical materialism as a 'science', towards a development of 'social philosophy' supplemented by empirical

[8] Jay, *The Dialectical Imagination*, pp. 11-17.

investigations. In 1932, the Institute ceased to issue the *Archives for the History of Socialism and the Workers' Movement*; its new review was innocently entitled *The Journal of Social Research*. In the short period before the Fascist counter-revolution of 1933, Horkheimer gathered a diverse and talented group of younger intellectuals about the Institute, of whom the most important were to be Marcuse and Adorno. Unlike Grünberg or Grossmann, Horkheimer had never been an overt member of any working-class party, although he had once admired Luxemburg and still remained politically radical, in a position critical of both the SPD and KPD. Marcuse, who had been a member of a soldiers' council in 1918, had retained some links with the organized workers' movement, in particular with the left of the SPD; in the last years before Hitler's seizure of power, he was a contributor to Hilferding's theoretical journal *Die Gesellschaft*. Adorno, on the other hand, as the cadet of the trio, had no personal ties at all to socialist political life. The scepticism of the new team at the Institute towards the prospects for class struggle in Germany, at a time when both the Social-Democratic and Communist Parties vaunted their confidence in the future, was shown at the outset of Horkheimer's tenure, when its funds were quietly transferred to Holland in 1931, and external offices established in Switzerland.[9]

The Nazi victory in 1933 thus exiled the Institute, but did not destroy it as a centre. Horkheimer was able to negotiate its formal transfer to the United States in 1934, where it was affiliated to Columbia University in New York; and before the outbreak of the Second World War all his closest colleagues had joined him in America. The emigration of the Institute to the USA transferred it into a political environment devoid of a mass working-class movement even formally committed to socialism, or of any substantial Marxist tradition. In its new milieu, the Institute as such gravitated steadily towards adaptation to the local bourgeois order, censoring its own past and present work to suit local academic or corporate susceptibilities, and conducting sociological surveys of a conventionally positivist character. To camouflage itself in its new habitat, a virtually complete retreat from politics was executed. Privately, Horkheimer and Adorno continued to maintain an acerbic hostility to US society, revealed after the war in

[9] Jay, *The Dialectical Imagination*, p. 26.

their joint work *Dialectic of Enlightenment* (prudently published in Holland), whose basic argument effectively equated North American liberalism and German fascism. The return of the Institute to Frankfurt again in 1949–50, however, could not alter the fundamental change in its social function and orientation that had supervened in the United States. For post-war West Germany was now politically and culturally the most reactionary major capitalist country in Europe – its Marxist traditions excised by Nazi chauvinism and Anglo-American repression, its proletariat temporarily passive and quiescent. In this milieu, in which the KPD was to be banned and the SPD formally abandoned any connection with Marxism, the depoliticization of the Institute was completed: whereas it had been an isolated enclave in the academic world in the USA, it was officially fêted and patronized in West Germany. The 'critical theory' advocated by Horkheimer in the thirties now explicitly renounced any link with socialist practice. Horkheimer himself ultimately collapsed into ignominious apologies for capitalism itself, in his retirement.[10] Adorno, on the other hand, who became director of the Institute in 1958, and produced its most powerful body of work after the Second World War, never took this path; his very aloofness from politics, always greater than that of his colleagues, preserved him from it. By contrast Marcuse, who had stayed behind in the USA, was to maintain an intransigently revolutionary position as an individual, amidst great intellectual and institutional isolation, in the fifties and sixties. But the objective strain of this situation had its price within his thought. Committed to the political ideals of classical Marxism, yet entirely removed from any active social force fighting for them, Marcuse in America came to theorize a structural 'integration' of the working class into advanced capitalism, and thus the insurmountability of the gulf between socialist thought – now inevitably become 'utopian' once again – and proletarian action in contemporary history. The rupture between theory and practice that had silently started in practice in Germany in the later twenties was clamantly consecrated in theory in the mid sixties, with the publication of *One-Dimensional Man*.

Prior to the victory of Nazism, Germany had been the only major

---

[10] See his interview in *Der Spiegel*, 6 January 1970.

European country outside Russia with a mass Communist Party. After it, France for the first time acquired a Communist movement of mass proportions, during the Popular Front period. After the Second World War, while the KPD was virtually eliminated from West Germany, the PCF became the majority organization of the working class in France. This dual change transformed the whole balance of Marxist culture within Europe. From the epoch of the Second International onwards, the French workers' movement – which in the early nineteenth century had led the continent in political militancy and intellectual creativity – had lagged theoretically well behind its counterparts in Eastern and Central Europe, or even in Italy. Marxism had never penetrated deeply into either the SFIO or CGT. The reasons for this cultural backwardness in the Third Republic were essentially two-fold: on the one hand, the strength of native pre-Marxist traditions (Proudhonism, Blanquism, Anarcho-Syndicalism) among the proletariat itself, and on the other hand the continuing vigour of bourgeois radicalism (of a late Jacobin type) which still anchored the local intelligentsia securely to their own class. Where a confluence of these two currents occurred, as in a leader like Jaurès, the result was a social doctrine of pronounced idealism and provincialism. No significant contribution to the great Marxist debates of the pre-1914 epoch was made in France. To all intents and purposes, *Capital* was a closed book to the French Socialist Party; significantly, no major theoretical work written after Marx and Engels was translated in France before the First World War. The victory of the Entente in 1918, upholding the dominance of the French bourgeoisie and sparing the French working class the ordeal of defeat, further delayed the conditions for the growth of Marxism as a real force in the country. The French Communist Party, after an apparently triumphal start in 1920, soon dwindled to relatively modest proportions, with a membership of some 50,000 for the rest of the decade; the intellectuals it attracted were mostly literary personalities with a sentimental rather than scientific relationship to the heritage of socialist ideas.

It was not until 1928 that the first cluster of younger intellectuals with a real interest in Marxism joined the Party. This group included Nizan, Lefebvre, Politzer, Guterman and Friedmann; it had crystallized in revolt against the sterility and parochialism of official French philosophy, and had originally possessed sympathies with surrealism.[11] Its entry into the PCF, however, coincided with the final Stalinization of the international Communist movement, during the Third Period. From the outset, therefore, it was subject to strict political constraints on its theoretical work. For by now, all central questions concerning the analysis of capitalist development and the conduct of the class struggle were the reserved domain, not even of the national party leadership in France, but of the Comintern in Russia itself. The field for intellectual activity within Marxism had thus greatly contracted, inside the ranks of the European Communist Parties. Politzer, after a pioneering attempt at a Marxist critique of psychoanalysis,[12] became little more than an obedient cultural functionary of the PCF. Nizan's polemical verve was steadily stifled by organizational pressures, until he finally rebelled against the Nazi-Soviet Pact and was expelled from the party.[13] Lefebvre alone maintained both a relatively high level and volume of written output, and public fidelity to the PCF. He was able to do so by a tactical innovation that was later to become widely characteristic of successor Marxist theorists in Western Europe: payment to Caesar what was due to Caesar – political loyalty, combined with intellectual work sufficiently dissociated from the central problems of revolutionary strategy to escape direct control or censorship. Lefebvre's major writings in the thirties were mainly philosophical in character, at a level of abstraction just containable within the limits of party discipline. The publication of his most important work, *Dialectical Materialism*, delayed for three years after its composition, was greeted by official suspicion;[14] in tone and concern, it can be situated somewhere between the earlier directness of Lukács, with its explicit appeals to 'history', and the contemporary evasiveness of Horkheimer, with its increasingly elusive appeals to 'critical theory'. Lefebvre, although

---

[11] For the background of this group, see Henri Lefebvre, *La Somme et Le Reste*, Paris 1959, pp. 389–414.

[12] *Critique des Fondements de la Psychologie*, Paris 1928. Politzer had witnessed the Hungarian Commune in his youth, suggesting a tenuous link with Central European Marxism.

[13] See Sartre's vivid essay in the re-edition of Nizan's *Aden Arabie*, Paris 1960; the two men were close friends.

[14] For this episode, see Lefebvre's autobiographical account in *La Somme et Le Reste*, p. 47.

read by Benjamin (with whom he shared a sympathy towards surrealism) in Paris,[15] remained an international isolate at the close of the thirties; within France itself, his example was a solitary one.

It was the German occupation of 1940–4 which overturned the whole political and cultural universe of the Third Republic, and for the first time produced the conditions for a generalization of Marxism as a theoretical currency in France. The PCF, which had grown to a mass party of over 300,000 members in the last years of the Popular Front, became the dominant popular force in the Resistance from 1941 onwards, and emerged enormously strengthened from the War. After 1945, its organizational paramountcy within the French working class was overwhelming. The result was a rapid growth in its power of intellectual recruitment and attraction. Politzer had been killed in the Resistance; Nizan had died at Dunkirk. Lefebvre remained the most distinguished and prolific philosopher in the Party for the next decade. For during this period, the increase in the mass of intellectuals drawn into the PCF yielded comparatively little new theoretical work within it, because it was largely neutralized by the extreme intensification of the cultural controls within the Party with the onset of the Cold War, and the violent enforcement of Zhdanovism by the PCF leadership at the height of it. Thus the major novel phenomenon of the first decade after the War was the impact of Marxism within the existentialist milieu that had first emerged during the Occupation, and which acquired wide cultural radiation after it, with the works of Sartre, Merleau-Ponty and De Beauvoir. This impact was mediated by the influence of Kojève, the first academic philosopher to introduce Hegel systematically into France before the war, and whose 'existential' interpretation of *The Phenomenology of Mind* provided an indirect passage for Sartre and Merleau-Ponty to Marxism after it.[16] In 1946,

[15] See Benjamin's essay *Eduard Fuchs, der Sammler und der Historiker*, in *Angelus Novus*, Frankfurt 1966, pp. 326, 341. Benjamin's contacts in Paris form an important subject for future research.

[16] Kojève's pre-war lectures were eventually published in 1947, as *Introduction à la lecture de Hegel*. Alexandre Kojève (Kozhevnikov) was born in Russia in 1902, and studied philosophy in Germany from 1921 to 1927, under the influence of Jaspers and Heidegger. He then went to France, where Alexandre Koyré, another Russian emigré, turned his interests to Hegel, on whom he lectured in succession to Koyré at the Ecole Pratique des Hautes Etudes from 1934 till the Second World War.

the two men founded an independent socialist journal, *Les Temps Modernes*, whose wide variety of philosophical, political, literary, anthropological and psychoanalytical contributions rapidly made it the most influential theoretical review in the country. Neither Merleau-Ponty nor Sartre were tempted to join the PCF, but both tried in succession to maintain an active revolutionary commitment alongside it, articulating political ideas that the Party itself refused to admit, without opposing or attacking it. This ambiguous relationship, founded on the belief that the bulk of the French working class was unshakeably organized by a party that suffocated intellectual work within it, finally led to the extraordinary attempt by Sartre in 1952–4 to make a direct theorization of the political practice of the PCF from outside it, in the series of essays entitled *The Communists and Peace*.[17] Naturally, no such 'excentric' unity of theory and practice proved possible. The Hungarian Revolt of 1956 led Sartre to a spectacular break with the PCF, and he thereafter developed his theoretical work outside any organizational frame of reference, as an individual philosopher and publicist avowedly without contact with the masses. Meanwhile, in the Communist Party itself, the repercussions of the Twentieth Party Congress of the CPSU and the Hungarian Revolt had finally driven Lefebvre into active opposition, and in 1958 he was expelled from it. These years saw the nadir of the PCF's political passivity during the Algerian War.

The limited liberalization of the party's internal régime in the sixties, however, revealed that new intellectual forces had been in hidden gestation within it. Already the publication of Cornu's serial biography of Marx and Engels, from 1955 onwards, had established a shift of the scholarly tradition of Mehring and Ryazanov to France.[18] But it was the appearance of the work of Louis Althusser, from 1960 to 1965, which signalled a decisive change in the level of intellectual debate within the party. For the first time, a major theoretical *system* was articulated within the organizational framework of French Communism, whose power and originality were conceded even by its most determined opponents. Althusser's influence spread very swiftly after

---

[17] Recently published in an English translation, London 1969.
[18] Auguste Cornu, *Karl Marx et Friedrich Engels*, Paris 1955–70: so far four volumes have appeared, covering the period up to 1846.

1965, both inside and outside the ranks of the PCF, giving him a unique position in the history of the party.[19] However, the paradox of this ascendancy has been its development against the grain of the political evolution of the PCF itself. The pronounced moderatism of Western Communism in the sixties, in fact, achieved its most developed expression in the party's programme for an 'advanced democracy' in France; while internationally the PCF distinguished itself by the degree of its hostility towards China and espousal of Russian positions in the Sino-Soviet conflict. Althusser's work, by contrast, defined itself as explicitly anti-humanist at a time when the official French party doctrine extolled the virtues of humanism as a common bond between contractual partners (communists, socialists, catholics) in the building of an advanced democracy, and the Soviet party was proclaiming 'Everything for Man' as a mass slogan; while his sympathies for China were thinly veiled. Thus, once again, there was marked torsion in the relationship between theory and party in the PCF: where previously the latter had stridently imposed 'orthodoxy' against the 'liberal' proclivities of the former, the roles were now reversed and the former mutely claimed rigorism against the laxity of the latter. In the new situation, however, the very liberalization of the PCF, to reassure its allies and partners, combined with the studied personal caution of Althusser to avert any frontal clash. In this respect, Althusser's position within the French party came to resemble that of Lukács in the Hungarian Party, after the Soviet intervention of 1956. In both cases, major intellectuals with a deep biographical tie to the Communist movement, refused to leave or break with it, making a tacit bargain with their party to keep silence on politics proper if their theoretical work (whatever its ultimate practical implications) was left relatively untouched. The viability of this mutual accommodation presupposed considerable independent prestige on the part of each theorist, making possible a tactical coexistence which it was in the interests of the party organization concerned not to terminate. The ambiguity and strain inherent in this type of bond were no less evident: particularly so in the case of Althusser, because of the lack of coercive constraints operative in the PCF in France.

[19] Althusser's two major works, *Pour Marx* and *Lire Le Capital*, appeared within a few months of each other in 1965.

The extraordinary scale and speed of the diffusion of Marxism in Italy after the Liberation, covering not only the growth of the PCI but also of the PSI and of wide unorganized sectors of the intelligentsia as well, had no comparison in any other European country. Combined with the post-war reception of historical materialism in France, it ensured that the main axis of Marxist culture after 1945 shifted from the Germanic to the Latin zone within Europe, for the first time in the century. But the development of Italian Marxism was to take a notably different course from that of French Marxism over the next two decades. Italy had possessed an indigenous Marxist tradition going back to the time of Engels in the late nineteenth century. Labriola's work had been inherited and continued in the next generation by Mondolfo, another ex-Hegelian philosopher who had in turn exercised a direct influence on Gramsci's generation.[20] The long interlude of fascism had then incubated the prison writings of Gramsci himself. These were now discovered and published for the first time in 1947–9. Their impact was enormous, both within the PCI itself and far outside it. The presence of this native Marxist heritage, culminating in the great work undertaken by Gramsci, thus helped to immunize Italian Communism against the most extreme ravages of the Cold War: Zhdanovism was resisted by the PCI to a much greater extent than by the PCF in France. The party leadership, still largely composed of men who had been Gramsci's contemporaries and colleagues, tempered the worst cultural repression typical of the Cominform period, and permitted a certain freedom of intellectual expression within the organization, provided that it was segregated from the political activity of the party. On the other hand, its posthumous canonization of Gramsci ironically served to sterilize the vitality of his theoretical bequest to Italian Marxism. The figure of Gramsci was converted into an official ideological icon of the party, invoked on every public occasion, while his actual writings were manipulated or neglected: twenty-five years after the end of the War, the PCI had not even produced a serious critical edition of his works. The mingled aromas of incense and dust surrounding the *Prison Notebooks* thus led to the unexpected result that the most important theoretical tendency that developed within Italian Marxism

[20] For the role of Mondolfo, see Christian Riechers, *Antonio Gramsci. Marxismus in Italien*, Frankfurt 1970, pp. 21–4.

after the Second World War represented a reaction against the whole philosophical filiation from Labriola to Gramsci.

The founder of the new school was Galvano Della Volpe, a philosopher who joined the PCI in 1944 and produced a series of influential works from 1947 to 1960. Della Volpe, like the majority of Italian academic intellectuals in the pre-war epoch, had compromised with fascism. Formally absolved from this past by his adherence to the PCI after the Badoglio coup, his record nonetheless disqualified him from acquiring any political authority within the party; while the same personal traits which had once led him to accept and justify the corporate State, subsequently inclined him towards consistent conformity to the policies of the leadership of the PCI. Thus while Della Volpe's theoretical orientation was manifestly divergent from the prevalent orthodoxy of the party, his own work lacked any autonomous political charge. The most eminent professional philosopher in the party, he was also in many ways the most marginal to it. No serious friction developed between Della Volpe and the PCI throughout his two decades of membership in it: equally, little ceremony was accorded him by the cultural apparatus of the party. Under his influence, however, a group of younger intellectuals emerged who formed the most coherent and productive school within the PCI – Pietranera, Colletti, Rossi, Merker, Cerroni and others. Of these, the most gifted and trenchant was Colletti, who joined the party in his mid-twenties in 1950. After the Twentieth Congress of the CPSU and the Hungarian Revolt, the theoretical journal of the PCI, *Società*, was editorially broadened in 1957 by the inclusion (among others) of Della Volpe and Pietranera, joined by Colletti in the following year. In this period, the philosophical themes of the school started to acquire political overtones among some of the younger members of the group. In particular, the philosophical insistence on the importance of 'determinate scientific abstraction', characteristic of Della Volpe's work, could be read to imply the need for an analysis of Italian society in terms of the 'pure' categories of developed capitalism, with correspondingly 'advanced' political objectives to be pursued by the working class within it. This contrasted with PCI orthodoxy, which emphasized the historically backward and hybrid character of Italian society, necessitating more limited demands of a 'democratic' rather than socialist type, as politically appropriate to it.[21] The theoretical tensions within *Società* eventually led to the suppression of the journal by the PCI in early 1962, followed by a full-scale philosophical debate in the party weekly *Rinascita* – launched with an arraignment of the Della Volpean school, to which Colletti replied with acerbity. Two years later, disaffected by the failure of any real democratization within the USSR or the Western Communist parties since 1956, Colletti left the PCI.[22] His main work in the next decade was produced outside any organizational framework.

Thus, from 1924 to 1968, Marxism did not 'stop', as Sartre was later to claim; but it advanced via an unending detour from any revolutionary political practice. The divorce between the two was determined by the whole historical epoch. At its deepest level, the fate of Marxism in Europe was rooted in the absence of any big revolutionary upsurge after 1920, except in the cultural periphery of Spain, Yugoslavia and Greece. It was also, and inseparably, a result of the Stalinization of the Communist Parties, the formal heirs of the October Revolution, which rendered impossible genuine theoretical work within politics even in the absence of any revolutionary upheavals – which it in turn contributed to prevent. The hidden hallmark of Western Marxism as a whole is thus that it is a product of *defeat*. The failure of the socialist revolution to spread outside Russia, cause and consequence of its corruption inside Russia, is the common background to the entire theoretical tradition of this period. Its major works were, without exception, produced in situations of political isolation and despair. Lukács's *History and Class Consciousness* (1923) was written in exile

[21] See Franco Cassano (ed.), *Marxismo e Filosofia in Italia*, Bari 1973, pp. 7–8, 14–19, 180–1. This volume includes the texts of the major theoretical debates within the PCI in the fifties and sixties, including the controversy of 1962 referred to below.

[22] [For this history, see now Colletti's own account, in 'A Political and Philosophical Interview', *New Left Review*, No. 86, July–August 1974, pp. 3–9. This remarkable text is of great importance for a whole range of theoretical and political problems discussed in this essay. A number of its conclusions, in fact, are similar to certain theses advanced here – although naturally invested with their own degree of authority. No other major thinker within the tradition of Western Marxism has revealed such lucidity about its nature and limits as Colletti. Needless to say, there is no reason to assume that he would assent to many of the particular arguments or judgements of this essay.]

in Vienna, while white terror raged in Hungary after the suppression of the Hungarian Commune. Gramsci's *Notebooks* were composed in gaol near Bari, after the definitive repression of the Italian working-class movement by triumphant fascism. The two most important works of the Frankfurt School were published at the worst nadir of political reaction in West Germany and the United States after the war: Adorno's *Minima Moralia* (1951) in the year that the formal process of banning the KPD started in West Germany, Marcuse's *Eros and Civilization* (1954) during the hysteria of McCarthyism in America. In France, Sartre's *Critique of Dialectical Reason* (1960) was published after the success of the Gaullist coup of 1958, and at the height of the Algerian War, when the mass of the French working class – led by the PCF – lay numbed and inert, while terrorist attacks by the OAS struck at the few individuals who actively resisted the war. It was in these years, too, that Althusser started to produce his first and most original studies: *Contradiction and Over-Determination* (1962), the most significant of these, coincided with the authoritarian installation of direct presidential rule and the full political consolidation of the Fifth Republic. This unbroken record of political defeat – for working-class struggle, for socialism – could not but have profound effects on the nature of the Marxism formed in this era.

At the same time, the Stalinization of the parties created by the Third International, from the late twenties onwards bureaucratically organized and ideologically subordinate to the policies of the USSR, left a further, distinctive imprint on it. The outcome of the Second World War, as has been seen, marked a pronounced shift in the geographical pattern of Marxism as an active culture in Europe, with the virtual disappearance of Communism as a living force among the working class of West Germany, and the emergence and dominance of mass Communist Parties in France and Italy. These differential situations led to a variety of responses to the problem of how to relate Marxist theory to proletarian politics, in the zones concerned, but no solution of it. Formal incorporation in working-class parties (Lukács, Della Volpe, Althusser), exit from them (Lefebvre, Colletti), fraternal dialogue with them (Sartre), or explicit renunciation of any connection with them (Adorno, Marcuse) were all equally incapable of uniting Marxist theory and mass struggle. For all these theorists, it may be said that the official Communist movement represented the central or sole pole of relationship to organized socialist politics, whether they accepted or rejected it. Two broad choices could be adopted, within the framework of this relationship. Either the theorist could enroll in a Communist Party and accept the rigour of its discipline. In this case, he could retain a certain nominal level of contact with the life of the national working class (to which despite everything the party was inevitably bound), and an at least philological continuity with the classical texts of Marxism and Leninism (whose study was mandatory within the party). The price of this proximity, however relative, to the realities of daily working-class struggle was silence about its actual conduct. No intellectual (or worker) within a mass Communist Party of this period, not integrated into its leadership, could make the smallest independent pronouncement on major political issues, except in the most oracular form. Lukács or Althusser exemplify this choice. The opposite option was to remain outside any party organization whatever, as an intellectual freelance. In this case, there was no institutional control on political forms of expression: but vice-versa there was also no anchorage within the social class for whose benefit theoretical work in Marxism alone has ultimate meaning. Sartre and Marcuse represent, in different ways, variants of this position. The former maintained an unmatched record of personal interventions in the cause of international socialism – writing major essays on France, Hungary, Algeria, Cuba, Congo, Vietnam, Czechoslovakia – yet without either any close knowledge of the classical heritage of Marxism, or impact on the working-class movement of his own country. The latter possessed a superior grounding in earlier Marxist traditions, and wrote full-length books dealing in their own oblique way with both the USA and USSR (*One-Dimensional Man* and *Soviet Marxism*), yet developed a theory effectively denying the industrial working class any active socialist potential at all. A final alternative was to abandon both any enrolment and any discourse within politics altogether: Adorno's stance in post-war Germany.

The consequence of this impasse was to be the studied silence of Western Marxism in those areas most central to the classical traditions of historical materialism: scrutiny of the economic laws of motion of capitalism as a mode of production, analysis of the political machinery of the bourgeois state, strategy of the class struggle necessary to overthrow it. Gramsci is the single exception to this rule – and it is the token of his greatness, which sets him apart from all other figures in this tradition. Logically: for he alone embodied in his person a revolutionary unity of theory and practice, of the type that had defined the classical heritage. The experience of the Italian workers' insurgency of 1919–20, and of organizational leadership within the PCI from 1924 to 1926, remained the creative sources of his thought, during the long imprisonment which sheltered him from the intellectual consequences of Stalinization outside Italy, while it slowly killed him. Even his writings, however, reveal the breakages and limits in the struggles of the class from which they were born, as well as the material circumstances of his captivity. After Gramsci, no other Marxist in Western Europe was ever to repeat the same order of attainment. The reduction of space for theoretical work to the constricted alternatives of institutional obedience or individual isolation crippled any possibility of a dynamic relationship between historical materialism and socialist struggle, and precluded any direct development of the main themes of classical Marxism. Within the Communist Parties, all discussion of the post-war imperialist economies, of the State systems of the West, and of the strategic conduct of class struggle, was strictly reserved for the bureaucratic apex of these organizations, itself conditioned by overall allegiance to official Soviet positions. Outside the ranks of organized Communism, there was no apparent foothold within the mass of the working class, from which to develop any intelligible revolutionary analysis or strategy – either because of Communist predominance in the local proletariat (France/Italy), or because of its overwhelmingly reformist loyalties (Germany/USA). The generation of theorists which had been formed by the dual experience of Fascism and the Second World War remained transfixed by it – whether they despaired of the working class altogether (the Germans, who knew no Resistance), or identified it inescapably with its Communist representation (the French or Italians, who had known a Resistance). It is probably significant that the youngest member of the group discussed here, Colletti, the only one whose main formation post-dates both Fascism and Resistance, should also be the only theorist of this tradition to have proved able to write on political and economic problems of the

post-war era, with both intellectual freedom and professional rigour –
since his departure from the PCI.[23] But even Colletti's contributions
have been essentially expository recapitulations of the balance-sheet of
classical debates, rather than substantive innovations in their own
right. For over twenty years after the Second World War, the
intellectual record of Western Marxism in original economic or
political theory proper – in production of major works in either field –
was virtually blank.

The institutional interdictions represented by the after-effects of
Fascism or the constraints of post-war Communism, however, were by
no means the sole reason for the sterility of Marxist theory in these
domains, within the West European theatre. For this was also the
epoch of an unparalleled objective consolidation of capital throughout
the advanced industrial world. Economically, the global dynamism of
the long boom of the fifties and sixties was greater than that of any
previous period in the history of capitalism. The general and massive
growth registered in this period effectively inaugurated a new phase in
the development of the mode of production as such, apparently con-
founding classical predictions of its impending decay or crisis, and
posing radically new problems for scientific analysis. The tradition of
Marxist economics which found its terminus in Sweezy's *Theory of
Capitalist Development* in 1942, had been effectively consigned to the
past at the end of that work, because of the visible success of the
Keynesian renovation of the US economy. When Sweezy and Baran
returned to the subject with a full-scale work twenty years later,
Monopoly Capital, the orthodox framework of Marxist economic
categories had been largely renounced by them.[24] The scale and force

[23] See in particular his essays *The Question of Stalin*, in *New Left Review*, No.
61, May–June 1970; and *Introduzione* in C. Napoleoni and L. Colletti (eds), *Il
Futuro del Capitalismo – Crollo o Sviluppo?*, Bari 1970, pp. LXXI–CXII.

[24] The relinquishment by Baran and Sweezy of the concept of surplus value,
the cornerstone of Marx's *Capital*, is well known. However, *Monopoly Capital*
(New York 1966) does not so much examine and reject concepts like surplus
value or the organic composition of capital by means of a direct critique, so
much as tacitly shift from them to vaguer analogies, often of somewhat Keynesian
provenance. It is in this sense that it is largely situated outside the terms and
procedures of classical Marxism. Baran, it should be noted, spent a formative year
(1930) in the ambience of the Institute of Social Research at Frankfurt; the latter
sections of *Monopoly Capitalism* reveal evident signs of its influence. Sweezy, for

of imperialist expansion of the forces of production in both its Atlantic and Pacific zones presented in its own right a formidable theoretical challenge to the development of historical materialism: the task, in all its dimensions, was never shouldered within the tradition of Western Marxism.[25] At the same time, the aftermath of the Second World War also saw the establishment, for the first time in the history of bourgeois rule, of representative democracy based on universal suffrage as the normal and stable structure of the State in all the main capitalist countries – West Germany, Japan, France, USA, England, Italy. The novelty of this political order as a durable and uniform system on an international scale is often forgotten in the Anglo-Saxon world, because of the relative length of its local traditions in England or the USA.[26] It can be judged by the absence of any central or cogent

his part, has recently emphasized that he does not regard the notion of 'surplus' in *Monopoly Capital* as in contradiction with that of 'surplus-value' in *Capital.* See his direct statement to this effect in *Monthly Review*, January 1974, pp. 31–2. In general, it may be said that since the publication of *Monopoly Capital* (Baran died shortly before), Sweezy's analyses of US capitalism in *Monthly Review* have been more orthodox in idiom.

[25] The enigmatic career of Michal Kalecki – a Pole – represents perhaps the closest engagement of European Marxism in this epoch with the major trans- formations of advanced capitalism. Born in Lodz in 1899, Kalecki – an engineer by education, with no formal qualifications in economics – anticipated most of the ideas of Keynes with his *Essay in Business Cycle Theory* in 1933, two years before the publication of *The General Theory of Employment, Interest and Money.* Emigrating to England via Sweden in 1935, he later became the first economist to predict the post-war pattern of counter-cyclical demand management in the West, with his article on 'The Political Aspects of Full Employment' (*The Political Quarterly*, 4, 1943). In 1955 he returned to Poland, where he occupied university and planning positions until shortly before his death in 1970. The ambiguity of Kalecki's work lay, of course, in the indeterminate nature of its relationship to Marxism. Further biographical research is needed on this. An anonymous writer in socialist journals in the semi-dictatorial Poland of the colonels in the thirties, Kalecki seems to have been criticized by the Polish CP for 'Luxemburgism', because of his preoccupation with the problems of effective demand and levels of investment. In England and America, his work – never cast in classical Marxist categories – was taken as a form of left-keynesianism. A final verdict has yet to be reached. Kalecki's achievement raises the question whether there has not existed a specifically Polish tradition of Marxist economics in this century, descending from Luxemburg – to which Grossman, Moszkowska and Kalecki may all, in different ways, have obliquely belonged.

[26] In England itself, the advent of universal suffrage dates only from 1929. In France, Italy and Japan it was introduced for the first time in 1945.

theorization of it within classical Marxism: the bourgeois-democratic State as such was never the object of any major work either by Marx, who never lived to see its realization, or by Lenin, whose enemy was an altogether distinct type of State in Tsarist Russia. The problems involved in developing a political theory capable of grasping and analysing the nature and mechanisms of representative democracy, as a mature form of bourgeois power, were thus scarcely less than those posed by the rapid advance of the world capitalist economy, in the first two decades after the war. They too went by default, within the mainstream of Marxist work in the West.

3
Formal Shifts

The progressive relinquishment of economic or political structures as the central concerns of theory was accompanied by a basic shift in the whole centre of gravity of European Marxism towards *philosophy*. The most striking single fact about the whole tradition from Lukács to Althusser, Korsch to Colletti, is the overwhelming predominance of professional philosophers within it. Socially, this change meant an ever increasing academic emplacement of the theory that was produced in the new epoch. In the time of the Second International, Luxemburg and Kautsky alike had been united in their scorn for *Kathedersozialisten* – 'professorial socialists' teaching in the universities, without party commitments. The Marxist intellectuals of the pre-First World War generation had never been integrated into the university systems of Central or Eastern Europe. The form of political unity between theory and practice which they represented was incompatible with any academic position. Instead, they typically taught at party or voluntary schools for workers, as one activity among others in a life of militancy. Hilferding and Luxemburg taught political economy at the SPD school in Berlin, while Lenin and Ryazanov lectured to Bolshevik workers in Longjumeau, and Bauer gave courses at the ÖSPD centre in Vienna. The first theorists of Western Marxism still knew this traditional pattern. Lukács taught in the radical Galileo Circle in Budapest during the First World War; Korsch lectured at the experimental Karl-Marx Schule in Berlin in the twenties. The creation of the Institute of Social Research in Frankfurt – an independent institution, yet affiliated to the local State university – marked a transitional phase in the Weimar Republic. After the end of the Second World War, however, Marxist theory had migrated virtually completely into the universities – precincts at once of refuge and exile from the political struggles in the world outside. In this period, Lukács, Lefebvre, Goldmann, Korsch, Marcuse, Della Volpe, Adorno, Colletti and Althusser all occupied university posts of professorial rank;[1] Sartre, rising into a university career, left it after success as a writer. In all cases, the discipline in which chairs were held was philosophy.

The external determinants which acted to move the main focus of Marxist theory from economics and politics towards philosophy, and its formal site from party assemblies to academic departments, were inscribed in the sombre history of the period. But this shift could never have occurred so generally and drastically, if there had not been a powerful internal determinant at work within Marxist culture itself as well. The decisive event here was the belated revelation of the most important early work of Marx – the Paris manuscripts of 1844. These were published for the first time in Moscow in 1932. Their immediate impact was muted by the victory in 1933 of Nazism in Germany – the country where their reception was likely to have been greatest at the time – and the onset of the purges in Russia in 1934. (Ryazanov, who had prepared the manuscripts for publication in his critical edition of the works of Marx and Engels, was dismissed from the Institute in Moscow just before they appeared.) Nevertheless, they made a deep and lasting impression on three thinkers at the time, independently. In his exile in Moscow, Lukács personally worked under Ryazanov in deciphering the manuscripts in 1931: the experience, by his own account, transformed his interpretation of Marxism permanently.[2] In Berlin, Marcuse greeted their publication with an essay in 1932 in *Die Gesellschaft* which started with the resounding declaration that they put 'the entire theory of "scientific socialism" on a new footing'; and stressed in particular his view that they demonstrated the key importance of the philosophical foundations of historical materialism,

[1] Lukács in Budapest; Korsch in New York; Marcuse in Brandeis and La Jolla; Lefebvre, Goldman and Althusser in Paris; Adorno in Frankfurt; Della Volpe in Messina; Colletti in Rome. Gramsci and Benjamin alone – the two victims of fascism – remained outside any university.

[2] See the interview, 'Lukács on His Life and Work', *New Left Review*, No. 68, July–August 1971, pp. 56–7; and the 1967 preface to *History and Class Consciousness* London 1971, p. XXXVI.

throughout all stages of the work of Marx.[3] In Paris, Lefebvre was responsible for the first translations from the Manuscripts into a foreign language – his edition of them, prepared in collaboration with Guterman, appeared in 1933; while the first major theoretical work to advance a new reconstruction of Marx's work as a whole in the light of the 1844 Manuscripts was Lefebvre's *Dialectical Materialism*, written in 1934–5.[4] It was in the period after the Second World War, however, that the full effects of the discovery of Marx's early works and their incorporation into the record of his thought, were themselves felt within the pattern of contemporary Marxism. In Italy, Della Volpe inaugurated his theoretical entry into historical materialism with the first translation and discussion in Italian of the new texts of the Young Marx – not only of the Paris Manuscripts, but more especially the *Critique of Hegel's Philosophy of Right* (1947–50).[5] In this case, too, the whole Della Volpean version of Marxism – which came to inspire a large school – hinged on a particular selection and interpretation of the early philosophical writings of Marx, albeit a very different one from those of Lukács, Marcuse or Lefebvre. In France, it was again the new texts of the Young Marx that largely drew Merleau-Ponty and Sartre towards Marxism after the Liberation: Sartre's first major approach to problems of Marxist theory, *Materialism and Revolution* (1947), appealed essentially to the authority of the Paris Manuscripts.[6] The peak of the influence of the philosophical writings of the early Marx was reached in the late fifties, when themes from them were diffused on the widest scale throughout Western Europe. So much so, that the first unequivocal rejection of these texts as constitutive of historical materialism at all – Althusser's initial essays – still perforce took them as the starting-point for any discourse within

[3] See Marcuse, *Studies in Critical Philosophy*, London NLB 1972, pp. 3–4, whose first essay is a translation of this key text, 'The Foundations of Historical Materialism'.

[4] *Le Matérialisme Dialectique*, first published in Paris 1939; English translation as *Dialectical Materialism*, London 1968, pp. 61–167 passim.

[5] See *La Teoria Marxista dell'Emancipazione Umana* (1945) and *La Libertà Communista* (1946), which focus mainly on the Paris Manuscripts, and *Per La Teoria d'un Umanesimo Positivo* (1947), which is centred on the *Critique of Hegel's Philosophy of Right*. Della Volpe's translations of both texts of Marx appeared in 1950.

[6] See *Literary and Philosophical Essays*, London 1955.

contemporary Marxism.[7] Even in negation, they defined the preliminary field of discussion. The very form of dismissal of Marx's early writings here, moreover, remained subject to the long-term alteration in the compass-points of Marxism which their discovery had rendered possible. For the positive theory developed by Althusser, against prior interpretations of Marx based on them, continued to be situated on a technically philosophical plane unknown before their advent.

Western Marxism as a whole thus paradoxically inverted the trajectory of Marx's own development itself. Where the founder of historical materialism moved progressively from philosophy to politics and then economics, as the central terrain of his thought, the successors of the tradition that emerged after 1920 increasingly turned back from economics and politics to philosophy – abandoning direct engagement with what had been the great concerns of the mature Marx, nearly as completely as he had abandoned direct pursuit of the discursive issues of his youth. The wheel, in this sense, appeared to have turned full circle. In fact, of course, no simple reversion occurred, or could occur. Marx's own philosophical enterprise had been primarily to settle accounts with Hegel and his major heirs and critics in Germany, especially Feuerbach. The theoretical object of his thought was essentially the Hegelian system. For Western Marxism by contrast – despite a prominent revival of Hegelian studies within it – the main theoretical object became Marx's own thought itself. Discussion of this did not, of course, ever confine itself to the early philosophical writings alone. The massive presence of Marx's economic and political works precluded this. But the whole range of Marx's oeuvre was typically treated as the source material from which philosophical analysis would extract the epistemological principles for a systematic use of Marxism to interpret (and transform) the world – principles never explicitly or fully set out by Marx himself. No philosopher within the Western Marxist tradition ever claimed that the main or ultimate aim of historical materialism was a theory of knowledge. But the common assumption of virtually all was that the *preliminary* task of theoretical

[7] In particular, 'Feuerbach's "Philosophical Manifestoes" ', 'On the Young Marx', and 'The 1844 Manuscripts of Karl Marx', in *For Marx*, London 1969.

research within Marxism was to disengage the rules of social enquiry discovered by Marx, yet buried within the topical particularity of his work, and if necessary to complete them. The result was that a remarkable amount of the output of Western Marxism became a prolonged and intricate Discourse on Method. The primacy accorded to this endeavour was foreign to Marx, in any phase of his development. The degree to which epistemological themes dominated this whole tradition can be seen in the titles of its characteristic works. Korsch's *Marxism and Philosophy* set out the basic rubric, at the very outset. The companion volume published by Lukács in the same year opened with an essay entitled *What is Orthodox Marxism?*, which concluded confidently that the term referred 'exclusively to *method*'.[8] This precept was thereafter to find faithful reflection in the obsessive methodologism of the works of the subsequent canon: books entitled successively *Reason and Revolution* (Marcuse), *Destruction of Reason* (Lukács), *Logic as a Positive Science* (Della Volpe), *The Problem of Method* and *Critique of Dialectical Reason* (Sartre), *Negative Dialectic* (Adorno), *Reading Capital* (Althusser).

The second-order nature of the discourse developed by these works – on Marxism, rather than in Marxism – had a further corollary. The language in which they were written came to acquire an increasingly specialized and inaccessible cast. Theory became, for a whole historical period, an esoteric discipline whose highly technical idiom measured its distance from politics. Marx's own work, of course, had by no means always been conceptually easy, for readers of his own time or posterity. But both his early philosophical texts and his late economic works (the two most difficult parts of his oeuvre) owed their initial system of terms to pre-existent theoretical ensembles – essentially Hegel and Ricardo – which they sought to criticize and surpass, by the production of new concepts clearer and closer to material reality: less 'hypostatized' (in the vocabulary of the young Marx), less 'theological' (in that of the mature Marx). Moreover, while never concealing the intrinsic difficulties for a reader of mastering any scientific discipline, Marx after 1848 always sought to present his thought in as simple and lucid a way as possible, to maximize its

---

[8] *History and Class Consciousness*, p. 1.

intelligibility to the working class for which it was designed. The care which he took for this purpose on the French translation of *Capital* is famous.

By contrast, the extreme difficulty of language characteristic of much of Western Marxism in the twentieth century was never controlled by the tension of a direct or active relationship to a proletarian audience. On the contrary, its very surplus above the necessary minimum quotient of verbal complexity was the sign of its divorce from any popular practice. The peculiar esotericism of Western Marxist theory was to assume manifold forms: in Lukács, a cumbersome and abstruse diction, freighted with academicism; in Gramsci, a painful and cryptic fragmentation, imposed by prison; in Benjamin, a gnomic brevity and indirection; in Della Volpe, an impenetrable syntax and circular self-reference; in Sartre, a hermetic and unrelenting maze of neologisms; in Althusser, a sybilline rhetoric of elusion.[9] Most of these writers were capable of communicating with clarity and directness. Some of them – Sartre, Adorno, Benjamin – were major literary artists in their own right. Yet virtually none of them spoke an even or uncontorted language in the major theoretical works for which they are usually remembered. Individual or subjective explanations cannot account for this recurrent, collective phenomenon. The case of Gramsci symbolizes, in its very exception, the historical rule that governed this general retreat of theory from classical Marxist parlance. The *Prison Notebooks*, the greatest work in this whole tradition, were written by a revolutionary leader of the working class, not by a professional philosopher, from a social background much poorer and lower than that of any important Marxist intellectual in Europe, whether Western or Eastern, before or after the First World War. Yet they contain numerous enigmas, many of them still unsolved by contemporary scholarship, because of the brute censorship and privation of imprisonment, which forced Gramsci

---

[9] The literary difficulty of these authors was to be frequently criticized in their own time. Gramsci's editing of *Ordine Nuovo* was attacked for its 'difficulty' by the French socialist newspaper *L'Humanité* in 1920, a charge which Gramsci replied to with a lengthy justification of his prose in *Ordine Nuovo*, 10 January 1920. Lukács was denounced for 'artistocratism of style' by Revai in 1949: see Josef Revai, *Lukács and Socialist Realism*, London 1950, pp. 18–19. Sartre's terminology was assailed with particular vigour by Lucien Sève, in 'Jean-Paul Sartre et la Dialectique', *La Nouvelle Critique*, No. 123, February 1961, pp. 79–82.

to resort to allusive codes rather than coherent expositions.[10] This physical reclusion, the consequence of defeat in class struggle, was to be a foreshadowed image of the isolation which surrounded the theorists who followed – freer than Gramsci, but remoter from the masses. The language of Western Marxism, in this sense, was subject to a wider historical censor: the gulf for nearly fifty years between socialist thought and the soil of popular revolution.

This long divorce, which shaped the theoretical *form* of Western Marxism, had another and arresting general effect on it. For everything happened as if the rupture of political unity between Marxist theory and mass practice resulted in an irresistible *displacement* of the tension that should have linked the two, towards another axis. In the absence of the magnetic pole of a revolutionary class movement, the needle of the whole tradition tended to swing increasingly away towards contemporary bourgeois culture. The original relationship between Marxist theory and proletarian practice was subtly but steadily substituted by a new relationship between Marxist theory and bourgeois theory. The historical reasons for this reorientation did not, of course, lie simply in the deficit of mass revolutionary practice in the West. Rather, the blockage of any socialist advance in the nations of advanced capitalism itself determined the total cultural configuration within these societies, in certain fundamental ways. Above all, the successful restabilization of imperialism, coupled with the stalinization of the communist movement, meant that major sectors of bourgeois thought regained a relative vitality and superiority over socialist thought. The bourgeois order in the West had not exhausted its historical life-span: its ability to survive two world wars, and to emerge for the next two decades economically more dynamic than ever before, was inevitably reflected in its capacity for cultural change and development. It still commanded the loyalty of the largest and best trained intellectual strata in the world, whose creative performance continued (with major national variations)

[10] Prison conditions do not, however, account for all the difficulties of Gramsci's notebooks. His language, as we have seen, had been criticized for undue complexity even in Turin; moreover, at least some of the riddles of the *Notebooks* are to be attributed to his own intellectual contradictions and uncertainties, in dealing with problems to which he never found an unequivocal or satisfactory answer.

to be substantial in field after field. This achievement naturally had certain fixed limits, dictated by the descendant position of capitalism on a global scale, in an epoch which despite everything saw a third of the world wrested from it. But the overall weakness of socialist culture, impaired or paralysed by the official repressions of Stalinism and the confinement of the international revolution to the backward zones of Eurasia, remained on balance much greater. After 1920, Marxism as a whole advanced less rapidly, in a large number of disciplines, than non-Marxist culture. This bitter reality exerted a central, bending pressure on the character of the work that was conducted within historical materialism in Western Europe.

The most striking single trait of Western Maxism as a common tradition is thus perhaps the constant presence and influence on it of successive types of European idealism. The range of inter-relationship between the two was always a complex one, involving both assimilation and rejection, loan and critique. The precise blend of response varied from case to case. But the basic pattern remained uncannily similar from the 1920s down to the 1960s. Lukács wrote *History and Class Consciousness* while still deeply under the intellectual impact of the sociology of Weber and Simmel, and the philosophy of Dilthey and Lask. In particular, its key categories of 'rationalization' and 'ascribed consciousness' were derived from Weber; its treatment of 'reification' was heavily marked by Simmel; while its hostility towards the natural sciences – something entirely foreign to all previous Marxist literature – was largely inspired by Dilthey and the outlook of German vitalism (*Lebensphilosophie*) generally.[11] Gramsci constructed his *Prison Notebooks* in large part as a sustained dialogue with and systematic critique of Croce – adopting the terminology and preoccupations of the idealist philosopher who then dominated the cultural scene in Italy, in particular his concern with ethico-political history;[12] while

[11] These influences are amply demonstrated in Gareth Stedman Jones's essay, 'The Marxism of the Early Lukács', *New Left Review*, No. 70, November–December 1971. Weber was a personal friend and colleague of Lukács before the First World War.

[12] For the complexity of Gramsci's attitude towards Croce, and his qualified admiration for the latter's category of 'ethico-political history', which he believed should be taken as an 'empirical canon' for historical research, see *Il Materialismo Storico*, Turin 1966, pp. 201–2, where Gramsci even compares

he also secondarily developed ideas and approaches of the literary critic De Sanctis, of an earlier generation. The collective work of the Frankfurt School was permeated from the thirties onwards with the concepts and theses of Freud's psychoanalysis, as the organizing reference of much of its own theoretical research. Marcuse's major study, *Eros and Civilization*, was to be expressly designated a 'philosophical enquiry into Freud', and its whole vocabulary of 'repression' and 'sublimation', 'reality principle' and 'performance principle', 'eros' and 'thanatos', moved within the latter's universe of discourse. The case of Sartre is a special one, in so far as he was himself the most eminent existentialist philosopher in France, formed by Heidegger and Husserl, before his passage to Marxism. He thus took with him into his Marxist writings his own intellectual past, with its distinctive instruments and inventions. The result was a conduit from many of the concepts of *Being and Nothingness* to those of the *Critique of Dialectical Reason*: among others, the notion of 'facticity' leading to 'scarcity', 'inauthenticity' to 'seriality', the instability of the 'for-itself-in-itself' to that of the 'fused group'.[13] At the same time, however, the two main prior sources of Sartre's original existentialist system remained active influences in his later thought: appeals or allusions to Husserl and Heidegger abound in his long study of Flaubert, published a decade after the *Critique of Dialectical Reason*. Althusser's work was conceived as an overt and radical polemic against his major predecessors – above all, Gramsci, Sartre and Lukács. But his theoretical system, too, owed many of its organizing terms to three disparate idealist thinkers: the notions of 'epistemological break' and 'problematic' were borrowed from Bachelard and Canguilhem – a philosopher and a historian of science, both of pronounced psychologistic bent; the ideas of a 'symptomatic reading' and a 'decentred structure' were taken from Lacan, a psychoanalyst combining Freudian orthodoxy with Heideggerian overtones; while the coinage of 'over-determination' itself, of

Croce to Lenin, as two theorists of hegemony, who both in their own way rejected economism.

[13] For a full account of the conceptual continuities between *Being and Nothingness* and the *Critique of Dialectical Reason*, see the admirable discussion in Frederic Jameson, *Marxism and Form*, Princeton 1971, pp. 230–74 – much the best critical analysis of the subject.

course, was imported directly from Freud.[14] These respective cultural correlates – governing the topographical position of the thought of Lukács, Gramsci, Marcuse, Sartre and Althusser – are only the most important and prominent such sets within the tradition of Western Marxism. Parallel relations can be found in nearly all of its representatives.[15] The central role played in Goldmann's work by the psychology of Piaget (with whom he worked in Switzerland during the war) is a typical instance. Even outside the framework of this tradition proper, the same rule has tended to hold: the relationship of Sweezy to Schumpeter within economic theory is a case in point.[16] Conversely, the influence of a single idealist thinker could extend to several different Marxist theorists. Bachelard, for example, not only inspired Althusser: he was also admired by Lefebvre, Sartre and Marcuse, who drew quite other lessons from his work.[17] Freud, above all, was a common discovery, not only of Adorno and Marcuse, but also of Althusser and Sartre – although again each adapted or interpreted his legacy in very diverse directions.[18] This constant concourse with contemporary thought-systems outside historical materialism, often avowedly antagonistic to it, was something unknown to Marxist theory before the First World War.[19] It was a specific and defining novelty of Western Marxism as such.

[14] For Althusser's own statements of his debts to Bachelard, Canguilhem and Lacan, see *For Marx*, p. 257, and *Reading Capital*, p. 16. Bachelard was Althusser's doctoral supervisor.

[15] The major exception is the Della Volpean school in Italy. Della Volpe himself borrowed extensively from Hjelmslev's linguistics for his aesthetic theory in *Critica del Gusto*, but the school as a whole remained relatively free of non-Marxist influences, compared with its homologues elsewhere. This absence was probably connected to the lack of major thematic innovations which also distinguished it, as will be seen later.

[16] See *The Theory of Capitalist Development*, p. ix.

[17] See *La Somme et Le Reste*, pp. 142–3; *Being and Nothingness*, London 1957, pp. 600–3; *Eros and Civilization*, London 1956, pp. 166, 209 and *One-Dimensional Man*, pp. 249–50. These authors were attracted essentially by Bachelard's poetics, rather than his epistemology.

[18] Compare Adorno, 'Sociology and Psychology', *New Left Review*, Nos 46–7, November 1967–February 1968; Marcuse, *Eros and Civilization*, passim; Althusser, 'Freud and Lacan', in *Lenin and Philosophy and Other Essays*, London NLB 1971; Sartre, *Between Existentialism and Marxism*, London NLB 1974, pp. 35–42.

[19] The impact of Darwinism in the age of the Second International provides

The patterned series of relationships running between major theorists of this tradition and modern thinkers within the arena of non-Marxist culture, constituted so to speak the horizontal axis of intellectual reference for Western Marxism. At the same time, however, it was also distinguished by a vertical axis of reference, of a type largely foreign to earlier Marxist traditions too. This was its invariable construction of a philosophical ancestry extending back *before Marx*. All the main theoretical systems of Western Marxism reveal the same spontaneous mechanism in this respect. Without exception, they had recourse to pre-Marxist philosophies – to legitimate, explicate or supplement the philosophy of Marx himself. This compulsive return behind Marx in quest of a prior vantage-point from which to interpret the meaning of Marx's work itself, was once again a suggestive index of the basic historical situation of Western Marxism. The new dominance of philosophers within the tradition was, as we have seen, one of the signs of the general sea-change that came over Marxist culture after 1920. The vertical lines of descent to which Western Marxism now laid claim, for Marx and for itself, owed much to this professional ascendancy within it. For Marx himself had left no systematic work of philosophy, in the classical sense, behind him. Abandoning his early philosophical theses to unpublished manuscripts, in his maturity he never ventured onto purely philosophical terrain again. Even his most important later statement of method, the 1857 Introduction to the *Grundrisse*, remained a programmatic fragment, never completed or edited for publication. The latent and partial nature of Marx's philosophical output had been compensated by Engels's later writings, above all the *Anti-Dühring*, for his immediate successors. But these fell into general discredit after 1920, when the incompatibility of some of

---

perhaps the nearest equivalent. However, the authority of evolutionism was that of a natural science, which did not impinge directly on the social domain of historical materialism. It could therefore be approved or adopted without any real internal modification of the latter. Even in the case of Kautsky, probably the theorist most susceptible to the influence of Darwinism, direct importations are not characteristic of his major pre-war work. A more extreme episode of this kind was, of course, the appeal of Mach for certain Bolshevik intellectuals, above all Bogdanov, which provoked Lenin to write *Materialism and Empirio-Criticism*. Here again, it was developments in the physical sciences which exerted a – transient – pull on trends within Marxism. No major figure of the third generation of classical Marxism was ever affected by them, however.

their central themes with the problems and findings of the natural sciences became increasingly obvious. Western Marxism, in fact, was to start with a decisive double rejection of Engels's philosophical heritage – by Korsch and Lukács in *Marxism and Philosophy* and *History and Class Consciousness* respectively. Thereafter, aversion to the later texts of Engels was to be common to virtually all currents within it, from Sartre to Colletti, and Althusser to Marcuse.[20] Once Engels's contribution was ruled out of court, however, the limitation of Marx's own legacy appeared more evident than before, and the need to supplement it more pressing. The resort to earlier philosophical authority within European thought for this purpose can be seen, in one sense, as a theoretical regression behind Marx. It is scarcely an accident that the peremptory sentence with which Marx himself closed his accounts with his intellectual forebears – 'Philosophers have only interpreted the world, in various ways; the point is to change it' – should have echoed so little within Western Marxism, whose philosophers were statutorily debarred from the revolutionary unity of theory and practice demanded by the eleventh thesis on Feuerbach. On the other hand, a single sentence cannot dispose of centuries of thought. Marx's mere dictum could never suffice by itself to furnish a new philosophy for historical materialism, or even to draw up the balance-sheet of older philosophies before it. Moreover, Marx's own philosophical culture was itself by no means an exhaustive one. Essentially steeped in Hegel and Feuerbach, it was not characterized by any very close acquaintance with Kant or Hume, Descartes or Leibniz, Plato or Aquinas, not to speak of other lesser figures. Thus in another sense, a chronological return behind Marx was not necessarily a philosophical recidivism, precisely because Marx himself had never directly assessed or surpassed all previous ethics, metaphysics, aesthetics, nor even touched on numerous basic issues of classical philosophy. There was, in other words, a certain legitimacy in the successive attempts made

[20] The single exception to this rule is the Italian Marxist Sebastiano Timpanaro, who has defended Engels's philosophical legacy with dignity and authority in his book *Sul Materialismo* (Pisa 1970, pp. 1–122). The calibre of Timpanaro's work more than entitles him to consideration in any comprehensive survey of Western Marxism in this epoch. However, it has been so expressly aimed against all other schools within the latter, and represents a position so much apart, that a simple

within Western Marxism to establish an intellectual ancestry reaching back behind Marx. For *any* creative development of Marxist philosophy as such would inevitably have had to move through a reconsideration of the complex cognitive history which Marx himself ignored or bypassed. The existing starting-points within the work of Marx itself were too few and too narrow for this not to be necessary. At the same time, the dangers involved in a prolonged recourse to pre-Marxist philosophical traditions need no emphasis: the overwhelming weight of idealist or religious motifs within them is well enough known.

The first major reinterpretation of Marxism to make central use of a pre-Marxist system to construct its own theoretical discourse was Lukács's treatment of Hegel in *History and Class Consciousness*. Hegel had never been widely studied in the Second International: as a rule, its leading thinkers had regarded him as a remote, but no longer relevant precursor of Marx, less significant than Feuerbach.[21] Lukács radically overturned this estimate, elevating Hegel for the first time to an absolutely dominant position in the pre-history of Marx's thought. The influence of this reassessment of Hegel was to be deep and lasting, for the whole subsequent tradition of Western Marxism – whether later thinkers assented or dissented from it. But Lukács's appeal to Hegel went much further than this genealogical attribution. For two of the most basic theoretical theses of *History and Class Consciousness* were derived from Hegel, rather than from Marx: the notion of the proletariat as the 'identical subject-object of history', whose class consciousness thereby overcame the problem of the social relativity of knowledge; and the tendency to conceive 'alienation' as an external objectification of human objectivity, whose reappropriation would be a return to a pristine interior subjectivity – permitting Lukács to identify the attainment by the working class of true consciousness

---

inclusion of it here might seem gratuitous. Yet even this intransigently original work has not escaped certain common determinations of Western Marxism. See below, Ch. 4 note 40.

[21] See Lukács's own comments in *History and Class Consciousness*, p. XXI. The major exception was Labriola, who had been a Hegelian philosopher himself before his encounter with Marxism. Hence the sudden revelation of the 'discovery' of Hegel by Lenin, after the discredit of the Second International, in 1916.

of itself with the accomplishment of a socialist revolution. Forty years later, Lukács was to describe these distinctive theses of *History and Class Consciousness* as an 'attempt to out-Hegel Hegel' himself.[22] However, the revaluation of Hegel's importance for Marxism that *History and Class Consciousness* initiated found many successors. Lukács himself later sought to rediscover fundamental categories of Marx's thought in that of Hegel, rather than to introduce Hegelian categories into Marxism. His study of *The Young Hegel* (1938) was a much more scholarly endeavour to establish a direct continuity between Hegel and Marx, based on Lukács's reading of the 1844 Manuscripts in Moscow, and on the role of economic concepts such as labour in the early writings of Hegel.[23]

Three years later, Marcuse published *Reason and Revolution* in New York, subtitled *Hegel and the Rise of Social Theory* – the first attempt at a Marxist analysis of the whole development of Hegel's thought, in all its phases, as the preparation and precondition of Marx's work. Marcuse's fidelity to this concept of Hegel never wavered. Adorno, much more critical than either Lukács or Marcuse of Objective Idealism as a 'philosophy of identity', nevertheless explicitly based his major work on the procedures of the *Phenomenology of Mind*: 'Hegel's method', he declared, 'schooled that of *Minima Moralia*.'[24] In France, on the other hand, while accepting the ascription of central importance to Hegel in Marx's formation, Sartre was to reverse its evaluation and exalt the antithetical contribution of Kierkegaard as a philosophical corrective to Hegel within Marxism. While holding that Marx himself had superseded the antinomy of Kierkegaard and Hegel, he argued that Marxism in the twentieth century had tended to become a petrified neo-Hegelianism, thereby revalidating the protest of existentialism in the name of individual experience against an all-encompassing objectivist system, which Kierkegaard had first uttered.[25] Sartre's own reconstruction of the historical process as such in the *Critique of Dialectical Reason* took as its irreducible starting-point the individual conceived in this sense, as the final term of any social class. Even after

[22] *History and Class Consciousness*, p. XXIII.
[23] *Der Junge Hegel* was not published until 1948, because of the War.
[24] *Minima Moralia*, London NLB 1974, p. 16.
[25] *The Problem of Method*, London 1963, pp. 8–14.

the *Critique*, the only philosopher to whom he dedicated a special study was Kierkegaard.[26]

In Italy, Della Volpe and his school were resolutely anti-Hegelian from the outset – both trenchantly negative in their appraisal of Hegel's philosophy itself, and positive in their assertion that Marx's thought represented a complete break with Hegel. Della Volpe himself construed Marx through a descent running from Aristotle through Galileo to Hume – all of whom he claimed had conducted critiques of hypostases in their time similar to that aimed by Marx at Hegel.[27] It was his pupil Colletti, however, who wrote the major systematic attack on Hegelianism to be produced within Western Marxism: *Hegel and Marxism*. This work was designed as a full-scale demonstration that Hegel was a Christian intuitive philosopher, whose basic theoretical purpose was the annihilation of objective reality and the depreciation of the intellect, in the service of religion; and who therefore was at the antipodes from Marx. By contrast, Colletti argued that the true philosophical predecessor of Marx was Kant, whose insistence on the independent reality of the objective world beyond all cognitive concepts of it, prefigured the materialist thesis of the irreducibility of being to thought. Kant's epistemology thus anticipated that of Marx, although the latter was never aware of the extent of his debt to it.[28] Similarly, for both Della Volpe and Colletti, Marx's political theory possessed a decisive antecedent of which he was unconscious: the work of Rousseau. Kant's philosophical limits had lain in his acceptance of the exchange principles of liberal-capitalist society: it was precisely these that Rousseau repudiated, in a radically democratic critique of the bourgeois-representative State which Marx was later in all essentials to do little more than repeat.[29]

[26] See the important essay, 'Kierkegaard: The Singular Universal', in *Between Existentialism and Marxism*, pp. 146–69.

[27] *Logica Come Scienza Positiva*, Messina 1950.

[28] *Hegel and Marxism*, London NLB 1973, especially pp. 113–38. In the epoch of the Second International, Mehring and others (Adler) had been attracted towards Kant's ethics, but no systematic philosophical construction of the type advanced by Colletti had ever connected the epistemology of Kant with that of Marx.

[29] See Della Volpe, *Rousseau e Marx*, Rome 1964, pp. 72–7; and for the most extreme statement of this view, Colletti's 'Introduction' to Karl Marx, *Early Writings*, Penguin/NLR Library, London 1974.

A no less drastic, but sharply contrasted, re-alignment of Marx occurred in the work of Althusser and his school. Less philologically explicit, it was substantively the most sweeping retroactive assimilation of all of a pre-Marxist philosophy into Marxism. In this case, the ancestor assigned to Marx was Spinoza. For Althusser, indeed, 'Spinoza's philosophy introduced an unprecedented theoretical revolution in the history of philosophy, probably the greatest philosophical revolution of all time.'[30] Nearly all the novel concepts and accents of Althusser's Marxism, apart from those imported from contemporary disciplines, were in fact directly drawn from Spinoza. The categorical distinction between 'objects of knowledge' and 'real objects' was taken straight from Spinoza's famous separation of *idea* and *ideatum*.[31] The hidden monism uniting the two poles of this dualism was likewise faithfully derived from Spinoza: the Althusserian 'general essence of production', common to both thought and reality, was none other than a translation of the Spinozan maxim *ordo et connexio idearum rerum idem est, ac ordo et connexio rerum* ('The order and connection of ideas is the same as the order and connection of things').[32] Althusser's radical elimination of the philosophical problem of the guarantees of knowledge or truth, again followed Spinoza's dictum *veritas norma sui et falsi* – the logical consequence of any

[30] *Reading Capital*, p. 102. The implicit primacy accorded to Spinoza over Marx did have a major precedent, in this case, within the Second International. Plekhanov believed that Marxism was essentially 'a variety of Spinozism', writing that 'The Spinozism of Marx and Engels is materialism in its modern form': *Fundamental Problems of Marxism*, London 1929, pp. 10–11. These formulations have been strongly attacked by Colletti, for whom 'Plekhanov was one of those who regarded Marx as a mere extension and application of Spinoza': see *From Rousseau to Lenin*, London NLB 1972, p. 71. In the USSR in the twenties, Deborin and his pupils followed Plekhanov in regarding Spinoza as 'Marx without a beard'. One point to be noted is that, while Marx was largely unfamiliar with the work of Kant or Descartes, he had read Spinoza closely in his youth: yet there is little sign that he was ever particularly influenced by him. Only a handful of references to Spinoza, of the most banal sort, can be found in Marx's work.

[31] *Reading Capital*, p. 40, is express on this point. For Spinoza, *Idea vera est diversum quid a suo ideato: nam aliud est circulus, aliud idea circuli* (*De Emendatio Intellectus*).

[32] Compare *For Marx*, p. 169, *Reading Capital*, p. 216; and *Ethica*, II, Proposition VII.

rigorous monism.[33] Similarly, the central concept of 'structural causality' of a mode of production in *Reading Capital* was a secularized version of Spinoza's conception of God as a *causa immanens*.[34] Above all, Althusser's passionate attack on the ideological illusions of immediate experience as opposed to the scientific knowledge proper to theory alone, and on all notions of men or classes as conscious subjects of history, instead of as involuntary 'supports' of social relations, was an exact reproduction of Spinoza's denunciation of *experientia vaga* as the source of all error, and his remorseless insistence that the archetypal delusion was men's belief that they were in any way free in their volition, when in fact they were permanently governed by laws of which they were unconscious: 'Their idea of freedom is simply their ignorance of any cause for their actions.'[35] Spinoza's implacable determinism ended with the conclusion that even in the least oppressive society, the sway of illusion could never be shaken off: 'Those who believe that a people, or men divided over public business, can be induced to live by reason alone, are dreaming of the poet's golden age or a fairy-tale.'[36] Althusser was to adapt this final tenet too: even in a communist society, men would still be immersed in the phantasms of ideology as the necessary medium of their spontaneous experience. 'All human societies secrete ideology as the very element and atmosphere indispensable to their historical respiration and life.'[37] The systematic induction of Spinoza into historical materialism by Althusser and his pupils was intellectually the most ambitious attempt to construct a prior philosophical descent for Marx, and to develop abruptly new theoretical directions for contemporary Marxism from it.[38] In only

[33] *Reading Capital*, pp. 59–60. 'Truth is the criterion both of itself and of falsehood': *Ethica*, II, Prop. XLIII, Scholium.

[34] *Reading Capital*, pp. 187–9. *Deus est omnium rerum causa immanens, non vero transiens* ('God is the immanent, not transient cause of all things'): *Ethica*, I, Prop. XVIII.

[35] *Haec ergo est eorum libertatis idea, quod suarum actionum nullam cognoscant causam*: see *Ethica*, II, Prop. XXXV, Scholium. The fourth part of the *Ethica* is, of course, entitled *De servitute humana, seu de affectum viribus* – 'On the slavery of man, or the power of the emotions', a central theme throughout Althusser's work, once the transcription of 'emotions' into 'ideology' is made. See *For Marx*, pp. 232–5, *Reading Capital*, p. 180.

[36] Spinoza, *Tractatus Theologico-Politicus*, I, 5.   [37] *For Marx*, p. 232.

[38] [Since the writing of this paragraph, Althusser has for the first time acknowledged his debt to Spinoza. See *Elements d'Autocritique*, Paris 1974, pp.

one important respect, did Althusser turn elsewhere for significant bearings in the history of philosophy. Spinoza's relative indifference to history led Althusser to supplement his ancestry of Marx with a secondary line of descent from Montesquieu, in a relationship very similar to that of Kant to Rousseau in Colletti's genealogy. Montesquieu's *Esprit des Lois* was credited by Althusser with the momentous discovery of the concept of a social totality 'determined in the last instance' by one preponderant level within it, later to be scientifically founded by Marx in *Capital*.[39]

These successive returns beyond Marx have been the most pronounced and influential instances within Western Marxism. They do not exhaust the list, however. Goldmann, as is well-known, selected Pascal as the key precursor of dialectical theory in *The Hidden God*.[40] Lefebvre in his youth opted for Schelling as a philosophical progenitor.[41] In a deeper and more subterranean way, Adorno and Horkheimer were probably also inspired by Schelling, in their introduction of the notion of a 'fallen nature' into Marxism.[42] Marcuse, for his part, appealed to Schiller's aestheticism for his conception of a future communist society.[43] In some cases, again, a single philosopher could draw tributes from several diverse thinkers within the Western Marxist tradition. Nietzsche, for example, anathema to Lukács, was paradoxically to be saluted by Adorno and Sartre, Marcuse and Althusser.[44] But perhaps the most telling evidence of an invisible

---

65–83. However his account of it remains vague and generic, characteristically lacking textual references and specific correspondences. It thus fails to reveal the real extent and unity of the transposition of Spinoza's world into his theoretical work. Further philogocial study would have little difficulty in documenting this.]

[39] *Politics and History*, London NLB 1973, pp. 52–3 ff.

[40] *The Hidden God*, London 1964, pp. 243–4, 251–2, 300–2. Goldmann had earlier selected Kant as the central precursor of the Marxist notion of totality: see *Immanuel Kant*, London NLB 1971.

[41] *La Somme et Le Reste*, pp. 415–24: this episode, not of great importance in itself for Lefebvre's later work, is in other ways particularly revealing for the wider pattern of this tradition. Lefebvre recounts that he and Politzer keenly felt the lack of any appropriate ancestry, and so consciously set out to try and find a suitable one for them, eventually alighting upon Schelling.

[42] The re-emergence of this occult notion in the culture of the German Left remains a problem for research. It probably first interested Ernst Bloch.

[43] *Eros and Civilization*, pp. 185–93.

[44] Compare Lukács, *Der Zerstorung der Vernunft*, Berlin 1953, pp. 244–317

regularity traversing the entire field of Western Marxism, however acute the internal contrasts and oppositions within it, is the case of Gramsci. For Gramsci was the one major theorist in the West who was not a philosopher, but a politician. No purely professional interest could have impelled him to seek a prior pedigree behind Marx. Yet he too organized his most original work centrally about a precursor – Machiavelli. For Gramsci, the compelling ancestor of the pre-Marxist past was necessarily not a classical philosopher, but a political theorist like himself. But the extent and type of Gramsci's borrowings from Machiavelli are fully homologous with those of other thinkers within Western Marxism. He too took both terms and themes directly from the anterior system of the Florentine into his own work. In the *Prison Notebooks*, the revolutionary party itself becomes a modern version of the 'Prince', for whose unitary power Machiavelli called. Reformism is interpreted as a 'corporative' outlook akin to that of the Italian cities, against whose divisive narrowness Machiavelli had inveighed. The problem of a 'historical bloc' between proletariat and peasantry is seen through the prefiguration of his plans for a Florentine popular 'militia'. The mechanisms of bourgeois rule are analysed throughout in the dual guises of 'force' and 'fraud', the two shapes of Machiavelli's Centaur.[45] The typology of State systems is derived from his triad of 'territory', 'authority' and 'consent'. For Gramsci, Machiavelli's thought 'too could be called "philosophy of praxis"'[46] – Gramsci's nomenclature for Marxism, in prison. Thus even the greatest, and least typical of its representatives, confirms the generative rules of Western Marxism.

The operative unity delimiting the field of Western Marxism as a whole, with its overall displacement of axes, did not, of course, preclude subjective divisions and sharp antagonisms within it. These, indeed, contributed to much of the internal vitality and variety of this tradition,

(the only extended treatment), with the comments in Adorno, 'Letters to Walter Benjamin', *New Left Review*, No. 81, September–October 1973, p. 72; Sartre, *Saint Genet*, London 1964, pp. 346–50; Marcuse, *Eros and Civilization*, pp. 119–24; Althusser, *Lenin and Philosophy*, p. 181.

[45] Gramsci, *Prison Notebooks*, London 1971, esp. 125–43, 147–8, 169–75.

[46] *Prison Notebooks*, p. 248.

once its external boundaries were historically set. It is characteristic of Western Marxism, however, that it never produced any accurate or adequate cartography of its own intellectual landscape. This absence was a logical consequence of one of the most striking and paradoxical features of the new theoretical culture that developed after 1920 – its *lack of internationalism*. This pattern, too, marked a radical departure from the canons of classical Marxism. It has been seen how Marx and Engels themselves corresponded and disputed with socialists all over Europe, and beyond it. The successor theorists of the Second International were rooted in their national political contexts much more firmly than the founders of historical materialism: but they too formed at the same time an integrated arena of international socialist debate. In the next generation after Marx and Engels, the reception of the work of Labriola provides perhaps the most eloquent example of the continental communication of the time. The first Marxist theorist to emerge in the politically backward and forgotten zone of Southern Europe, Labriola became known with extraordinary speed from Paris to St Petersburg. His first major essay, indeed, was commissioned by Sorel for *Le Devenir Social* in France in 1895; within a year, Kautsky's journal *Die Neue Zeit* in Germany had registered and welcomed it; in 1897 Plekhanov published a long review of Labriola's writings in *Novoe Slovo* in Russia; a few months later, Lenin was urging his sister to translate them into Russian; and in 1898, a Russian translation duly appeared. The next generation of Marxists if anything formed an even more internationalist community of thinkers and militants, whose passionate theoretical debates were in large measure informed by thorough and intimate study of each other's works. The controversy over Luxemburg's *Accumulation of Capital* is an impressive example. It was this background, of course, which made the disciplined creation of the Third International a culmination of, as well as a rupture with, the previous historical experience of the working-class movement on the continent.

With the victory of 'Socialism in One Country' in the USSR, however, followed by the progressive bureaucratization of the Comintern, and the final nationalist perspectives adopted by European Communism during and after the Second World War, the dominant framework of Marxist discussion underwent a fundamental change. It now increasingly proceeded, not merely at a distance from political militancy, but also from any international horizon. Theory gradually contracted into national compartments, sealed off from each other by comparative indifference or ignorance. This development was all the stranger, in that the overwhelming majority of the new theorists – as we have seen – were academic specialists at the highest levels of their respective university systems, in principle ideally equipped with capacities of both language and leisure for serious study and knowledge of intellectual systems outside their own nation. Yet in fact, the philosophers of this tradition – complex and recondite as never before in their own idiom – were virtually without exception utterly provincial and uninformed about the theoretical cultures of neighbouring countries. Astonishingly, within the entire corpus of Western Marxism, there is not one single serious appraisal or sustained critique of the work of one major theorist by another, revealing close textual knowledge or minimal analytic care in its treatment. At most, there are cursory aspersions or casual commendations, both equally ill-read and superficial. Typical examples of this mutual slovenliness are the few vague remarks directed by Sartre at Lukács; the scattered and anachronistic asides of Adorno on Sartre; the virulent invective of Colletti against Marcuse; the amateur confusion of Althusser between Gramsci and Colletti; the peremptory dismissal by Della Volpe of Althusser.[47] All these are merely incidental comments in works whose main purpose lies quite elsewhere. There is no case within Western Marxism of a full theoretical engagement or conflict of one thinker or school with another – let alone any overall command of the international range of the tradition as such. Even in the cases of a relationship between mentor and disciple, this is true: Goldmann's allegiance to the work of the early Lukács, for example, was never accompanied by the slightest critical interest or study of his later work. The result of this generalized parochialism and blankness towards extra-national bodies of thought was to prevent any coherent or lucid self-awareness of the lay-out of Western Marxism as a whole. The unfamiliarity of each

---

[47] Sartre, *The Problem of Method*, pp. 21, 37–9, 52–4; Adorno, *Negative Dialectic*, London 1973, pp. 49–51; Colletti, *From Rousseau to Lenin*, pp. 128–40; Althusser, *Reading Capital*, pp. 134–8; Della Volpe, *Critica dell'Ideologia Contemporanea*, Rome 1967, pp. 25–6n, 34–5n, 37n.

theorist with the next kept the real system of relations and distinctions between them in opaque obscurity.

This is not to say that there were no attempts at all to draw up clear battle-lines within the field of Western Marxism. At least two such were made in the sixties, by Althusser and Colletti respectively. Both were based on an indiscriminate amalgamation of all other systems than their own into a single philosophic bloc and a rejection of this ensemble as descended from and vitiated by Hegel, together with a claim that their own work alone reconnected directly with Marx. Otherwise, however, the two accounts of the development of Marxism since the 1920s were mutually incompatible, since Althusser's categories explicitly included Colletti in the Hegelian tradition he repudiated, while Colletti's logic assigned Althusser to the Hegelian heritage he denounced. Of these retrospective constructions, Althusser's interpretation was broader and more comprehensive. For him, the works of Lukács, Korsch, Gramsci, Sartre, Goldmann, Della Volpe and Colletti were all classifiable as variants of 'historicism': an ideology in which society becomes a circular 'expressive' totality, history a homogeneous flow of linear time, philosophy a self-consciousness of the historical process, class struggle a combat of collective 'subjects', capitalism a universe essentially defined by alienation, communism a state of true humanism beyond alienation.[48] Most of these theses – Althusser argued – were derived from Hegel, mediated through Feuerbach and the writings of the Young Marx: the scientific theory of historical materialism was founded on a radical break with them, accomplished by Marx in *Capital*. Colletti's reconstruction, by contrast, was narrower in focus, if even longer in reach: for him, the early Lukács, Adorno, Marcuse, Horkheimer and Sartre were united by a common attack on science and denial of materialism, inherent in the claim that contradiction is a principle of reality rather than of reason – while the dialectical materialism to which the later Lukács and Althusser subscribed was merely a naturalistic version of the same concealed idealism. Both were derived from Hegel's metaphysical critique of the intellect, whose aim was the philosophical annihilation of matter.[49] This critique

[48] See *Reading Capital*, pp. 119–43.
[49] *Marxism and Hegel*, pp. 181–98. Althusser's espousal of the dialectics of

had been fatally misunderstood and adopted by Engels in the *Anti-Dühring* – founding a line of descent that was to be a complete departure from the rational and scientific materialism of Marx, exemplified in the logical method of *Capital*.

What validity can be accorded to either of these two presentations? It is clear enough that both the Della Volpean and Althusserian schools have been distinguished by certain common features which set them off from other systems within Western Marxism. Their hostility towards Hegel – developed earlier and more thoroughly in the Della Volpean system – demarcates them most obviously in a tradition otherwise predominantly drawn towards Hegel. Together with this, they shared an aggressive re-emphasis on the scientific character of Marxism, on the pre-eminence of *Capital* within Marx's work itself, and on the cardinal subsequent importance of Lenin's political thought. They both represented a vehement reaction against prior theoretical trends which negated or ignored many of the claims of the classical tradition. But these characteristics do not suffice to divide the whole field of European Marxism since 1920 into two antithetical camps. The simple polarities proposed by Althusser or Colletti are much too crude and cavalier, based on far too little comparative study, to provide any serious guide to the complex constellation of philosophical trends within Western Marxism, including their own. It would not even be accurate to speak of a more subtle or continuous spectrum, rather than a stark polarity, of systems. For the attitudes of individual theorists have often coincided or overlapped in disconcerting ways, from very diverse starting-points, precluding their alignment along any single band of philosophical location. The irreconcilability of the typologies offered by Colletti and Althusser is itself an indication of the logical aporia of both. Thus the theme of alienation was branded as arch-Hegelian by Althusser, and its rejection regarded as a precondition of scientific materialism: yet Colletti, whose attack on Hegel was more radical and more documented than that of Althusser, retained the concept of alienation as central to the work of the mature Marx, and to historical materialism as a science. Conversely, Colletti concentrated

nature as the one valuable element to be salvaged from Hegel, once it is re-baptized 'process without subject', situates him squarely within the field of Colletti's critique: see *Lenin and Philosophy*, pp. 117–19.

his most intense fire on the dialectics of matter in Hegel, as the religious touchstone of his idealism, and most baneful legacy to later socialist thought: yet Althusser actually singled out the same aspect of Hegel's work as the one viable kernel of scientific insight inherited from it by Marxism.

Moreover, the criss-crossing of lines extends well beyond these two protagonists. Much of Althusser's system was constructed against that of Sartre, locally dominant in France at the turn of the sixties; while most of Colletti's polemic was directed against the Frankfurt School, temporarily dominant in Italy in the late sixties. Neither appears to have had any close acquaintance with the main adversary of the other, with the result that each was unaware of certain diagonal similarities with them. Colletti's growing preoccupation with the duality of Marxism as 'science or revolution', theory both of the objective laws of capitalism and of the subjective capacity of the proletariat to overthrow the mode of production of which it is itself a structural part,[50] was in fact very close to the basic methodological starting-point of Sartre's enquiry. The involuntary correspondences between Althusser and Adorno – apparently the remotest possible pair of theorists – was more striking still. The Frankfurt School was from the outset of its formation more saturated with Hegelian influence than any other in Europe. Adorno's Marxism represented, by the sixties, an extreme version of its renunciation of any discourse on classes or politics – precisely the objects given formal primacy by Althusser's Marxism. Yet Adorno's *Negative Dialectic*, first developed in lectures in Paris in 1961 and completed in 1966, reproduces a whole series of motifs to be found in Althusser's *For Marx* and *Reading Capital*, published in 1965 – not to speak of others in Colletti's *Hegel and Marxism* published in 1969. Thus, among other themes, Adorno explicitly affirmed the absolute epistemological primacy of the object; the absence of any general subject in history; the vacuity of the concept of the 'negation of the negation'. He attacked philosophical concentration on alienation and reification as a fashionable ideology, susceptible to religious usage; the cult of the works of the Young Marx at the expense of *Capital*; anthropocentric conceptions of history,

[50] See, for example, *From Rousseau to Lenin*, pp. 229–36.

and the emollient rhetoric of humanism accompanying them; myths of labour as the sole source of social wealth, in abstraction from the material nature that is an irreducible component of it.[51] Adorno was even to echo exactly Althusser's precepts that theory is a specific type of practice ('theoretical practice'), and that the notion of practice must itself be defined by theory. 'Theory is a form of practice' wrote Adorno, and 'practice itself is an eminently theoretical concept'.[52] The defiant theoreticism of these pronouncements, effectively suppressing the whole material problem of the unity of theory and practice as a dynamic bond between Marxism and mass revolutionary struggle, by proclaiming their lexical identity at the outset, can be taken as a general *motto* of Western Marxism in the epoch after the Second World War. They indicate the underlying ground shared by the most disparate intellectual positions within it.

For, of course, the theoretical systems of Althusser and Adorno were otherwise notoriously dissimilar in problematic and orientation. The curious intersection of certain significant themes in their oeuvres is merely evidence that a vague binary contrast between Hegelian and anti-Hegelian schools is wholly inadequate to define the exact locations of the different schools within Western Marxism, or the inter-relations between them. The very multiplicity of the philosophical filiations discussed above – including not only Hegel, but Kant, Schelling, Spinoza, Kierkegaard, Pascal, Schiller, Rousseau, Montesquieu and others – precludes any such polar alignment. The collateral links of each theorist with variant sectors of contemporary bourgeois culture further complicate the problem of the affinities and antagonisms between them. These in turn were conditioned and regulated by diverse national political situations. In other words, it is perfectly evident that each individual system in this tradition has received the impress of a *plurality* of determinations, deriving from different horizons and levels of the social and ideological structures of its own time and the past, producing a wide heterogeneity of theories – inside the parameters

---

[51] See *Negative Dialectic*, pp. 183–4, 304, 158–60; 190–2, 67, 89, 177–8. It should be noted that Adorno's insistence on the primacy of the object is at least as strenuous as Colletti's, rendering the latter's generic attacks on the Frankfurt School in this respect largely otiose.

[52] *Stichworte*, Frankfurt 1968, p. 171; *Negative Dialectic*, p. 144.

of the basic historical conjuncture delimiting the tradition as such. There is no space here to explore the real distribution of relationships within this field, in all its complexity. For present purposes, it is more important to consider the salient originality of each system vis-à-vis the classical legacy of historical materialism of the preceding epoch. For in any balance-sheet of the record of Western Marxism, the development of new concepts or emergence of new themes provides the most critical gauge of its nature and power as a tradition.

Thematic Innovations

Some general facets can be discerned at once. Western Marxism, as we have seen, was progressively inhibited from theoretical confrontation of major economic or political problems, from the 1920s onwards. Gramsci was the last of its thinkers to broach central issues of class struggle directly in his writings. He too, however, wrote nothing about the capitalist economy itself, in the classical sense of analysing the laws of motion of the mode of production as such.[1] After him, an equivalent silence typically shrouded the political order of bourgeois rule, and the means of overthrowing it, as well. The result was that Western Marxism as a whole, when it proceeded beyond questions of method to matters of substance, came to concentrate overwhelmingly on study of *superstructures*. Moreover, the specific superstructural orders with which it showed the most constant and close concern were those ranking 'highest' in the hierarchy of distance from the economic infrastructure, in Engels's phrase. In other words, it was not the State

---

[1] Gramsci's silence on economic problems was complete. Yet, ironically and mysteriously, one of his closest and most life-long friends was Piero Sraffa – who mediated his correspondence with the PCI outside Italy during the final years of his imprisonment, and was probably the last man to talk over international politics with Gramsci, a few months before his death in 1937. There is a certain symbolism in this strange relationship between the greatest Marxist political thinker in the West and the most original economic theorist of the post-war epoch, with its combination of personal intimacy and intellectual separation. There appears to have been no remote connection between the universes of their respective works. Sraffa's eventual critique of neo-classical economics was to be more rigorous and damaging than anything achieved within the field of Marxism itself. Yet this signal achievement was accomplished by a return, beyond Marx, to Ricardo, and the system which emerged from it was scarcely less inclement for the theory of value in *Capital*.

or Law which provided the typical objects of its research. It was culture that held the central focus of its attention. Above all, within the realm of culture itself, it was *Art* that engaged the major intellectual energies and gifts of Western Marxism. The pattern in this respect is arresting. Lukács devoted the largest part of his life to work on literature, producing a serried file of critical studies on the German and European novel – from Goethe and Scott to Mann and Solzhenitsyn, culminating in a massive general *Aesthetics* – his longest and most ambitious published work.[2] Adorno wrote a dozen books on music, including both global analyses of the musical transformations of the twentieth century and interpretations of individual composers such as Wagner or Mahler, besides three volumes of essays on literature; he too completed his oeuvre with an overall *Aesthetic Theory*.[3] Benjamin's most significant theoretical legacy within Marxism was an essay on *Art in the Age of its Mechanical Reproduction*, and his major critical achievement in the thirties was a study of Baudelaire.[4] His accompanying concern was the work of Brecht.[5] Goldmann's principal work was an analysis of Racine and Jansenism – *The Hidden God*, which at the same time set out a general canon of literary criticism for

[2] *Aesthetik*, Berlin/Neuwied 1963. The most important works of Marxist literary criticism so far translated into English are *Studies in European Realism* (1950), *The Historical Novel* (1962), *The Meaning of Contemporary Realism* (1963), *Essays on Thomas Mann* (1964), *Goethe and His Age* (1967), *Solzhenitsyn* (1970); all but the first have been published by Merlin Press, which has also translated the pre-Marxist *Theory of the Novel* (1971).

[3] *Aesthetische Theorie*, Frankfurt 1970. Of the major musical studies, only *Philosophy of Modern Music* (London 1973) has so far been translated into English. The three volumes of *Noten zur Literatur* were published in Germany (Berlin and Frankfurt am Main) 1958–61.

[4] See *Illuminations*, pp. 219–53; and *Charles Baudelaire: A Lyric Poet in the Era of High Capitalism*, London NLB 1973.

[5] Benjamin was, of course, a close interlocutor of Brecht in exile. Brecht's own aesthetic thought, while obviously of great intrinsic importance in the history of European Marxism in his time, was always subordinate to his authorial practice as a dramatist, and therefore falls somewhat outside the scope of this essay. For Brecht's dual relationship to Benjamin and Lukács, see *Understanding Brecht*, pp. 105–21, and the essays translated in *New Left Review*, No. 84, March–April 1974 ('Against Georg Lukács'). Adorno's criticisms of Benjamin and Brecht, for their part, may be found in the texts translated in *New Left Review*, No. 81, September–October 1973 ('Letters to Walter Benjamin') and *New Left Review*, No 87/8, September–December 1974 ('Commitment'). These complex exchanges form one of the most central debates in the cultural development of Western Marxism.

historical materialism; his other writings explored the modern theatre and novel (Malraux).[6] Lefebvre in turn wrote a *Contribution to Aesthetics*.[7] Della Volpe, for his part, produced another full-scale aesthetic theory, *Critique of Taste*, besides essays on films and poetry.[8] Marcuse wrote no separate work on any specific artist, but systematically keyed aesthetics as the central category of a free society, in which 'art as form of reality' would finally shape the objective contours of the social world itself – a theme common to both *Eros and Civilization* and *An Essay on Liberation*.[9] Sartre's first encounter with Marxism coincided with his publication of *What is Literature?*; during the transition towards his own work within Marxist theory, his major output was on Genet, while also writing on Mallarmé and Tintoretto[10]; and when he had finally completed his passage to Marxism, he spent the next decade on a monumental study of Flaubert – conceived on a scale larger than the sum of all his earlier philosophical works combined.[11] Gramsci represents, as usual, a related but distinct case within this gallery. He wrote at considerable length on Italian literature in the *Prison Notebooks*,[12] but the primary object of his theoretical enquiry was not the realm of art, but the total structure and function of culture for systems of political power in Europe, from the Renaissance onwards. Thus his most profound and original investigations were institutional analyses

[6] *Pour une sociologie du roman*, Paris 1964.

[7] *Contribution à l'esthétique*, Paris 1953.

[8] *Critica del Gusto*, Milan 1960; *Il Verosimile Filmico*, Rome 1954.

[9] His most explicit statement can be found in his essay 'Art as a Form of Reality', in *New Left Review*, No. 74, July–August 1972.

[10] The studies of Mallarmé and Tintoretto, of which only fragments have been published, were in fact full-length books: see M. Contat and M. Rybalka, *Les écrits de Sartre*, Paris 1970, pp. 262, 314–15.

[11] *L'idiot de la famille*, Vols I–III, Paris 1971–2. There is a strange likeness between Sartre's work on Flaubert, and Benjamin's on Baudelaire, for all the contrast between the gigantism of the one and the miniaturism of the other. Benjamin's study was to be divided into three parts: Baudelaire himself as an allegorist; the social world of Paris in which he wrote; and the commodity as a poetic object synthesizing the meaning of both poet and capital. Sartre's study was also designed in a tripartite scheme: the subjective formation of Flaubert's personality; the Second Empire as the objective field of his reception as an artist; and *Madame Bovary* as the singular historical unity of the two.

[12] The volume *Letteratura e Vita Nazionale* is the longest in the Einaudi edition of the Prison Notebooks; but it includes Gramsci's early theatre criticism, before his imprisonment.

of the historical formation and division of intellectuals, the social nature of education, and the role of mediate ideologies in cementing blocs between classes. Gramsci's whole work was unremittingly centred on superstructural objects, but unlike any other theorist in Western Marxism he took the autonomy and efficacy of cultural superstructures as a *political* problem, to be explicitly theorized as such – in its relationship to the maintenance or subversion of the social order. Althusser too, finally, left the shores of method for substantive analysis only to explore exclusively superstructural questions: his lengthiest essay of this type was on ideology and education, its starting-point overtly derived from Gramsci; shorter texts discussed theatre or painting (Brecht or Cremonini), and the nature of art; while the only developed application of his ideas outside the field of philosophy proper to appear under the imprint of his personal authority has been a theory of literature.[13] The cultural and ideological focus of Western Marxism has thus remained uniformly predominant from first to last. Aesthetics, since the Enlightenment the closest bridge of philosophy to the concrete world, has exercised an especial and constant attraction for its theorists.[14] The great wealth and variety of the corpus of writing produced in this domain, far richer and subtler than anything within the classical heritage of historical materialism, may in the end prove to be the most permanent collective gain of this tradition.

At the same time, however, the major intellectual systems within Western Marxism have typically also generated specifically new theoretical themes, of wider import to historical materialism as a whole. The mark of these conceptions is their radical novelty to the classical legacy of Marxism. They can be defined by the absence of any indication or anticipation of them in the writings of either the young or the old Marx, or the work of his heirs in the Second International. The

[13] See 'Ideology and Ideological State Apparatuses', 'Cremonini, Painter of the Abstract', 'A Letter on Art', in *Lenin and Philosophy and Other Essays*; 'The "Piccolo Teatro": Bertolazzi and Brecht', in *For Marx*; and Pierre Macherey, *Pour une théorie de la production littéraire*, in Althusser's *Théorie* series, Paris 1966.
[14] It is significant that the only work of real quality ranging widely over Western Marxism as a whole, should be an aesthetic study: Frederic Jameson's *Marxism and Form*.

pertinent criterion here is not the validity of these innovations, or their compatibility with the basic principles of Marxism: it is their originality. A critical evaluation of the merits of each is not the task of these considerations, whose limits it would exceed. For the moment, it will be enough to isolate the most significant conceptual departures from precedent in the development of Western Marxism. Any such attempt must inevitably be to some extent arbitrary in its selection: particularly within the narrow scope of this essay, there can be no question of providing any exhaustive survey.[15] But certain distinctive themes stand out unmistakably in the theoretical array under discussion. They can be taken as a minimum count of the *sui generis* contributions of the tradition in question.

In this respect, first and foremost comes Gramsci's notion of *hegemony*. The term itself was derived from the Russian socialist movement, where Plekhanov and Axelrod had been the first to employ it, in strategic discussions of the future leadership by the working class of a revolution in Russia.[16] Gramsci's adoption of the term in effect transformed it into something like a new concept altogether in Marxist discourse, designed precisely to theorize the political structures of capitalist power that did not exist in Tsarist Russia. Recalling Machiavelli's analyses of force and fraud and tacitly inverting them, Gramsci formulated the concept of hegemony to designate the decisively greater strength and complexity of bourgeois class rule in Western Europe, which had prevented any repetition of the October Revolution in the advanced capitalist zones of the continent. This hegemonic system of power was defined by the degree of consent it obtained from the popular masses which it dominated, and a consequent reduction in the scale of coercion needed to repress them. Its mechanisms of control for securing this consent lay in a ramified network of

[15] It will be seen that the major systems which yielded no radically new departures from the canon of earlier Marxist theory are those founded by Della Volpe and Lukács. In both cases, this was related to closer textual fidelity to the writings of Marx himself (for better or worse?). Development of themes such as those of alienation or reification in the young Lukács do not qualify as genuine innovations, however widespread they became in much later Western Marxism, since they pervade the Young Marx.

[16] The evolution and significance of the concept of hegemony will be discussed at length elsewhere, in a forthcoming essay on Gramsci in *New Left Review*.

cultural institutions – schools, churches, newspapers, parties, associations – inculcating passive subordination in the exploited classes, via an ensemble of ideologies woven from the historical past and transmitted by intellectual groups auxiliary to the dominant class. Such intellectuals, in turn, could be either annexed by the ruling class from earlier modes of production ('traditional'), or generated within its own social ranks ('organic') as a new category. Bourgeois rule was further buttressed by the allegiance of secondary allied classes, welded into a compact social bloc under its political leadership. The flexible and dynamic hegemony exercised by capital over labour in the West through this stratified consensual structure, represented a far harder barrier for the socialist movement to overcome than it had encountered in Russia.[17] Economic crises, of the type which earlier Marxists had seen as the central lever of revolution under capitalism, could be contained and withstood by this political order. It permitted no frontal attack by the proletariat on the Russian model. A long and difficult 'war of position' would be necessary to contend with it. With this set of conceptions, Gramsci alone among its thinkers directly sought to find a theoretical explanation of the basic historical impasse that was the origin and matrix of Western Marxism itself.

Gramsci's theory of hegemony possessed another peculiarity within this tradition, too. It was based, not only on personal participation in contemporary political conflicts, but also on an extremely close, comparative enquiry into the European past. In other words, it was the product of scientific study of empirical material, in the classic sense in which this was practised by the founders of historical materialism. This was not to be true of any other major thematic innovation in Western Marxism. All the others were to be speculative constructions, in an older philosophical sense: a priori conceptual schemes for the understanding of history, not necessarily inconsistent with empirical evidence, but always undemonstrated by it in their mode of presentation. Characteristically, these conceptions have lacked any concrete grid of periodization, articulating them to straightforward historiographical categories of the sort that Gramsci carefully respected. The most sweeping and unexpected theory of this type was the vision of

[17] Among the key passages in Gramsci setting out these ideas, see in English translation, *Prison Notebooks*: pp. 229–39, 52–8, 5–14.

the relationship between *man and nature* developed by the Frankfurt School. Its origins go back to the philosophy of Schelling, who in mid-career had adopted a counter-evolutionist metaphysic, in which all recorded history was seen as a regression from a higher to a lower state of 'fallen nature', after an original 'contraction' of divinity from the world, and prior to an eventual 'resurrection' of nature with the reunification of deity and universe.[18] This religio-mystic doctrine was adapted and transformed by Adorno and Horkheimer into a secular 'dialectic of enlightenment'. The classical Marxist view of the march of history, from primitive communities to capitalism, had emphasized the increasing control of man over nature with the development of the forces of production as a progressive emancipation of human society from the tyranny of natural necessity (*Naturnotwendigkeit*); the fruits of this liberation were confiscated by successive exploiting classes through the social division of labour, but with the advent of communism would be reappropriated by the producers themselves to create at last a society of generalized abundance, whose final mastery of nature would be the token of the 'realm of freedom'. Adorno and Horkheimer converted this affirmative conception into a radically interrogative, or even negative one. For them, the original rupture of man with nature, and the subsequent process of his growing ascendancy over it, brought no necessary progress in human emancipation. For the price of domination over nature, of which man himself was inseparably a part, was a social and psychic division of labour that inflicted ever greater oppression on men, even as it created ever greater potential for their liberation. Subordination of nature proceeded *pari passu* with consolidation of classes, and hence subordination of the majority of men to a social order imposed as an implacable second nature above them. The advance of technology hitherto only perfected the machinery of tyranny.

[18] Schelling: 'Does not everything announce a sunken life? Did these mountains grow as they now are? Did the ground that supports us rise to its present level, or fall back to it? . . . Oh not those debris of primeval human magnificence, for which the curious traveller visits the wastes of Persia or the deserts of India, are the true ruins! The whole earth is an enormous ruin, whose animals dwell in it as ghosts, and men as spirits, and where many hidden forces and treasures are held fast as if by unseen powers or magic spells'. *Werke*, IV Erg. Bd., Munich 1927, p. 135.

At the same time, the structure of reason as the precondition of civilization was erected on the repression of nature in man himself, creating the psychological split between ego and id which made possible the rational control of his spontaneous impulses. The instrumental refinement of reason into logic and science steadily reduced the natural world outside man to mere quantified objects of manipulation, erasing the distinction between subsistent things and cognitive concepts to an operational identity. The return of the repressed that was the fatal consequence of this suppression of nature eventually achieved philosophical form in the Enlightenment, when Nature itself became inversely identified with Reason; and finally its political form in Fascism, when brute barbarism took its revenge on the civilization that had secretly preserved it, in a savage vengeance of degraded nature over reason.[19] The refinement of industrial technology too was to culminate in the possibility of planetary self-destruction: all its artefacts were subject to annihilation by explosion or pollution of the elements. A liberated society would thus cease to pursue any presumptuous quest: its historical goal would be, not domination of nature, but *reconciliation* with it. This would mean abandonment of the cruel and hopeless attempt to dictate an identity of man and nature, by the subjugation of the latter to the former, for an acknowledgement of both the distinction and relation between them – in other words, their vulnerable *affinity*.[20] The 'fall' of nature would then at last be redeemed, without and within men: but their non-identity would still preclude any harmony free of contradiction between them.

This basic thematic was common to the Frankfurt School as a whole. Marcuse, however, gave a special inflection to it. In his work, both nature and society acquired more precise and programmatic references. For Marcuse, directly following Freud, the instinctual nature in man was essentially sexual libido – Eros. Over and above the original repression necessary for primitive man to struggle against want and to achieve civilization, postulated by Freud, the structure of class society generated successive historical forms of 'surplus repression' derived from inequality and domination. The technological wealth of advanced

[19] Adorno and Horkheimer, *Dialectic of Enlightenment*, London 1973, esp. pp. 81–119, 168–208.
[20] *Minima Moralia*, p. 155–7; *Negative Dialectic*, pp. 6, 191–2; 270.

capitalism, however, now made possible the end of surplus repression, by the inauguration of a socialism of abundance.[21] Therewith the pleasure principle (coupled with its obverse principle of avoidance of pain, called Thanatos by Freud) could at last concord with the reality principle of the external world, once the constraints of alienated labour were abolished. Human and natural emancipation would then coincide in erotic liberation. This would mean not merely a polymorphous release of sexuality, but a diffusion of libidinal investment into work and social relations themselves – that would confer on every practice of a pacified existence the sensuous qualities of aesthetic play. In this Orphic world beyond the 'performance principle' of capitalism, sublimation would cease to be repressive; erotic gratification would flow freely through all social life; man and nature would be finally attuned in a harmonious unity of subject and object.[22] This affirmation sharply distinguished Marcuse from Adorno, whose work contained no such sensuous solution. However, for Marcuse the actual course of history negated its possible outcome: contemporary capitalism realized the very inverse of a true libidinal emancipation – the 'repressive de-sublimation' of a commercialized and pseudo-permissive sexuality, damming up and deadening any rebellion of erotic impulses at a deeper level. A comparable fate had befallen art – once critical, now incorporated and neutralized in a culture celebrated by established reality. Technology, in turn, had ceased to contain the hidden possibility of an alternative society: the very advance of modern forces of production had become an involution, perpetuating existing relations of production. The abundance it had created now merely permitted capitalism to integrate the proletariat into a monolithic social order of oppression and conformity, in which it had lost all consciousness of itself as a separate and exploited class.[23] Democracy was thus now the normal guise of domination, tolerance a suave agency of manipulation within a homogeneous system in which the masses – deprived of any dimension of negative consciousness – mechanically elected their own masters to rule them.

The central use of Freud to develop a new theoretical perspective

[21] *Eros and Civilization*, pp. 35–7, 151–3.
[22] *Eros and Civilization*, pp. 164–7, 194–5, 200–8, 116.
[23] *One-Dimensional Man*, 60–78, XVI, 19–52.

within Marxism, evident in Marcuse's work, was paradoxically also to characterize Althusser's. The selection of concepts from psycho-analysis, and their transformation, were however in this case very different. Where Marcuse adapted Freud's metapsychology to for-mulate a new theory of instincts, Althusser took over Freud's concept of the unconscious to construct a new theory of *ideology*. Althusser's radical break with the traditional conceptions of historical materialism lay in his stark claim that 'ideology has no history', because it is – like the unconscious – 'immutable' in its structure and operation within human societies.[24] The authority for this dictum was, by analogy, the work of Freud, for whom the unconscious was 'eternal'. Ideology, for Althusser, was a set of mythical or illusory representations of reality, expressing the imaginary relationship of men to their real conditions of existence, and inherent in their immediate experience: as such, it was an unconscious system of determinations, rather than a form of consciousness as ordinarily conceived. The permanence of ideology as a lived medium of delusion was, in turn, a necessary consequence of its social function, which was to *bind* men together into society, by adapting them to the objective positions allocated them by the dominant mode of production. Ideology was thus the indispensable cement of social cohesion, in every period of history. For Althusser, the reason why it was inescapable as an ensemble of false beliefs and representations was that all social structures were by definition opaque to the individuals occupying posts within them.[25] Indeed, the formal structure of all ideology was an invariant inversion of this real relation-ship between social formations and the individuals within them: for

---

[24] *Lenin and Philosophy*, pp. 151–2.

[25] See in particular, 'Théorie, Pratique Théorique et Formation Théorique. Ideologie et Lutte Ideologique' – a text hitherto published in book-form only in Spanish translation: *La Filosofía como Arma de la Revolución*, Córdoba 1968, pp. 21–73. Its theses are unequivocal: 'In a society without classes, just as in a class society, ideology has the function of securing the *bond* between men in the ensemble of the forms of their existence, the relation of individuals to their tasks fixed by the social structure . . . the deformation of ideology is socially necessary as a function of the very nature of the social whole: more specifically, as a function of its determination by its structure which renders this social whole opaque to the individuals who occupy a place in it determined by this structure. The repre-sentation of the world necessary to social cohesion is necessarily mythical, owing to the opacity of the social structure.' pp. 54–55.

the key mechanism of any ideology was always to constitute individuals as imaginary 'subjects' – centres of free initiative – *of* society, so as to assure their real subjection *to* the social order, as blind supports or victims of it. Religion in general (the 'binding' of man to God), and Christianity in particular, provided in this respect the archetypal model of the effects of all ideology – to instil the illusions of liberty the better to ensure the workings of necessity. Spinoza had furnished a complete account of this characteristic operation of ideology, and precisely with respect to religion, earlier and more thoroughly than Marx. But the unconscious nature of ideology could today be related and articulated to Freud's scientific concept of the psychic unconscious, itself 'initiated' by the forms of ideology peculiar to the family as an objective structure.[26] Finally, the transhistorical statute of ideology as the unconscious medium of lived experience, meant that even in a classless society, its system of errors and delusions would survive to give vital cohesion to the social structure of communism itself. For this structure, too, will be unseen and impermeable to the individuals within it.[27] The science of Marxism will never coincide with the lived ideas and beliefs of the masses under communism.

The conclusions of the work of Sartre have certain curious similarities of undercurrent to those of Althusser. But the defining theme of Sartre's system, that distinguishes it from any other, is set by the category of *scarcity*. The term itself was coined by the Italian *philosophe* Galiani during the Enlightenment, who first formulated value as a ratio between utility and scarcity (*rarità*) in any economic system;[28] this technical notion of scarcity passed marginally into Ricardo, was virtually ignored by Marx, and eventually re-emerged as a central category in neo-classical economics after him. Sartre's use of the term,

[26] *Lenin and Philosophy*, pp. 160–5.

[27] *For Marx*, p. 232; *La Filosofía como Arma de La Revolución*, p. 55.

[28] Fernando Galiani, *Dalla Moneta*, Milan 1963 edition: 'Value, then, is a ratio; and this is composed of two ratios, expressed by the names of utility and scarcity' (p. 39). His use of the term was subsequently adopted by Condillac. For Ricardo: 'Possessing utility, commodities derive their exchangeable value from two sources: from their scarcity, and from the quantity of labour required to obtain them'. *The Principles of Political Economy and Taxation*, London 1971 edition, p. 56. In practice, however, Ricardo largely ignored scarcity in his theory of value, since he regarded it as pertinent only to very restricted categories of luxury goods (statues, paintings, wines).

however, had virtually nothing in common with that of Galiani. For the latter believed that the original condition of mankind was one of abundance: the most useful objects were also the most plentiful in nature.[29] Marx was more ambiguous in his allusions to the question. But while occasionally suggesting a primitive state of scarcity,[30] he more usually implied an original profusion of nature relative to the paucity of human needs before the advent of civilization.[31] Moreover, his theory of value contained no reference to scarcity whatever, unlike even the nominal mention of it by Ricardo. For Sartre, on the other hand, scarcity was the 'fundamental relation' and 'condition of possibility' of human history, both the contingent starting-point and the 'passive motor' of all historical development. No original unity between man and nature existed: on the contrary, the absolute fact of scarcity determined nature as the 'negation of man' from the start, and history conversely as an anti-nature. The struggle against scarcity generated the division of labour and so the struggle between classes: therewith man himself became the negation of man. Violence, the incessant oppression and exploitation of all recorded societies, is thus internalized scarcity.[32] The harsh dominion of the natural world over

[29] 'With marvellous providence, this world is so constituted for our good that utility, generally speaking, never coincides with scarcity. . . . The things needed to sustain life are so profusely spread over the whole of the earth, that they have no, or relatively little, value': *Dalla Moneta*, p. 47.

[30] In *The German Ideology*, Marx wrote that 'the development of the forces of production is an absolutely necessary practical premise because without it *scarcity* is merely generalized (*nur der Mangel verallgemeinert*), and with destitution (*Notdurft*) the struggle for necessities would begin again and all the old filth would necessarily be reproduced'. See *Werke*, Vol. 3, pp. 34–5. This passage was to be recalled by Trotsky in his analysis of the reasons for the rise of Stalinism in Russia, which made scarcity (*nuzhda*) a central category of its explanation: see *The Revolution Betrayed*, New York 1965, pp. 56–60.

[31] The most representative statement is perhaps to be found in the *Grundrisse*: 'Originally the free gifts of nature [are] abundant, or at least merely to be appropriated. From the outset, naturally arisen association (family) and the division of labour and cooperation correspond to it. For needs themselves are scant at the beginning.' *Grundrisse*, London 1973, p. 612. At the same time, of course, for both Marx and Engels the 'realm of freedom' was defined by material super-abundance beyond the 'realm of necessity' that governed both pre-class and class societies.

[32] *Critique de la Raison Dialectique*, pp. 200–24. The analogy often drawn between Sartre and Hobbes is unfounded. For Hobbes, as for Galiani, nature

men, and the divided antagonism of their efforts to transform it to assure their lives, typically give rise to serial collectivities – inhuman ensembles of which each member is alien to each other and himself, and in which the ends of all are confiscated in the total outcome of their actions. Such series have always been the predominant form of social coexistence in every mode of production to date. Their formal antithesis is the 'fused group', in which all men are members of one another, united in a fraternal enterprise to achieve a common goal, in and against the milieu of scarcity. The supreme example of a fused group is a mass movement at the apocalyptic moment of a successful revolutionary rising.[33] But to maintain itself in existence, pursuing an unequal combat in a world of violence and want, such a group must endow itself with organizational inertia and functional specialization in its turn, losing its fraternity and dynamism to become an 'institutional' group. Petrification and dispersion now await it: the next step is to transfer the unity of the group upwards into a 'sovereign' authority above it, to achieve a vertical stabilization. The State is the final embodiment of such a sovereignty, and its invariable structure is that of a restricted, authoritarian summit manipulating dispersed series beneath it, through a bureaucratic hierarchy and repressive terror. With its consolidation, the active group that originally created it is degraded once more to serialized passivity.[34] If groups and series compose the 'formal elements of any history' for Sartre, the real history of social classes charts the complex combinations or conversions of these forms into each other. Classes themselves, however, never constitute fused groups as a whole: they are always an unstable compound of apparatuses, groups and series – in which the latter will normally predominate. Thus the classical Marxist notion of the 'dictatorship of the proletariat' was an impossible contradiction in terms, a bastard compromise between active sovereignty and passive seriality.[35] For no class as such can coincide with a State: political power cannot be exercised by the entire working class, and the State is

---

assured an original *plenty* to man, who had to do little more than receive it as the fruits of the earth. See *Leviathan*, XXIV, London 1968 edition, pp. 294–5.

[33] *Critique de la Raison Dialectique*, pp. 306–19 ff, 384–96 ff.

[34] *Critique de la Raison Dialectique*, pp. 573–94, 608–14.

[35] *Critique de la Raison Dialectique*, pp. 644, 629–30.

never a real expression of even the majority of it. The bureaucratization and repression of all post-revolutionary States produced by history so far is thus linked to the very nature and condition of the proletariat as a social ensemble, so long as global scarcity and class divisions exist. Bureaucracy remains an ineliminable accompaniment and adversary of socialism in this epoch.

It will be seen that the successive innovations of substantive theme within Western Marxism, just surveyed, reflected or anticipated real and central problems that history posed to the socialist movement during the half-century after the First World War. Gramsci's absorbing concern with hegemony prefigured the consensual stabilization of the capitalist State in the West, two decades before it emerged as a durable and general phenomenon. Many of Adorno's preoccupations with nature, at the time an apparently perverse by-way of the Frankfurt School, suddenly reappeared in the later widespread debate over ecology within the imperialist countries. Marcuse's analyses of sexuality presaged the institutional breakdown of erotic constraints and sensibility, emancipation as enervation, characteristic of much bourgeois culture after the mid-sixties. Althusser's main excursus on ideology was directly inspired by the wave of revolts within the higher educational system of the advanced capitalist world in the same period. Sartre's treatment of scarcity schematized the universal crystallization of bureaucracy after every socialist revolution in the backward countries, while his dialectic of series and groups anticipated much of the formal course of the first mass rising against capitalism in the developed countries after the Second World War (France in 1968). The relative value or adequacy of the solutions advanced by each system to the problems under its purview is not our concern here. It is rather the collective direction of the theoretical innovations peculiar to Western Marxism that needs to be elicited and emphasised.

For, no matter how otherwise heteroclite, they share one fundamental emblem: a common and latent *pessimism*. All the major departures or developments of substance within this tradition are distinguished from the classical heritage of historical materialism by the darkness of their implications or conclusions. In this respect, between 1920 and 1960, Marxism slowly changed colours in the West.

The confidence and optimism of the founders of historical materialism, and of their successors, progressively disappeared. Virtually every one of the significant new themes in the intellectual muster of this epoch reveals the same diminution of hope and loss of certainty. Gramsci's theoretical legacy was the prospect of a long war of attrition against an immensely stronger structure of capitalist power, more proof against economic collapse than had been envisaged by his predecessors – a struggle with no final clarity of outcome visible. His own life indefectibly bound to the political fate of the working class of his time and nation, Gramsci's revolutionary temper was tersely expressed in the maxim 'pessimism of the intellect, optimism of the will': once again, it was he who alone consciously perceived and controlled what was to be the timbre of a new and unheralded Marxism. The pervasive melancholy of the work of the Frankfurt School lacked any comparable note of active fortitude. Adorno and Horkheimer called in question the very idea of man's ultimate mastery of nature, as a realm of deliverance beyond capitalism. Marcuse evoked the utopian potentiality of the liberation of nature in man, only to deny it the more emphatically as an objective tendency in reality, and to conclude that the industrial working class was itself perhaps absorbed past recall within capitalism. The pessimism of Althusser and Sartre had another but no less grave horizon, the very structure of socialism itself. Althusser declared that even communism would remain opaque as a social order to the individuals living under it, deceiving them with the perpetual illusion of their liberty as subjects. Sartre rejected the very idea of a true dictatorship of the proletariat as an impossibility, and interpreted the bureaucratization of socialist revolutions as the ineluctable product of a scarcity whose end remained inconceivable in this century.

These specific substantive theses were accompanied by general accents and cadences absolutely unwonted in the earlier history of the socialist movement. These too were in their own less direct way unmistakable signs of the profound alteration of historical climate that had now come over Marxism in the West. No previous thinker within the tradition of historical materialism could have written in tones and images such as those that Adorno or Sartre, Althusser or Gramsci, were to use. The Frankfurt School's constant perception of history was best expressed by Benjamin, in a language that would have been virtually incomprehensible to Marx or Engels: 'This is how one pictures the angel of history. His face is turned towards the past. Where we perceive a chain of events, he sees one single catastrophe which keeps piling wreckage upon wreckage and hurls it in front of his feet. The angel would like to stay, awaken the dead, and make whole what has been smashed. But a storm is blowing from Paradise; it has got caught in his wings with such violence that the angel can no longer close them. This storm irresistibly propels him into the future to which his back is turned, while the pile of debris before him grows skyward. This storm is what we call progress.' Benjamin typically wrote, of the annals of all class struggle: '*Even the dead* will not be safe from the enemy if he wins; and this enemy has not ceased to be victorious.'[36] Gramsci meanwhile, in prison and defeat, summed up the vocation of a revolutionary socialist in the epoch with a desolate stoicism: 'Something has changed, fundamentally. This is evident. What is it? Before, they all wanted to be the ploughmen of history, to play the active parts, each one of them to play an active part. Nobody wished to be the "manure" of history. But is it possible to plough without first manuring the land? So ploughman and manure are both necessary. In the abstract, they all admitted it. But in practice? Manure for manure, as well draw back, return to the shadows, into obscurity. Now something has changed, since there are those who adapt themselves "philosophically" to being "manure", who know that is what they must be. . . . There is not even the choice between living for a day like a lion, or a hundred years as a sheep. You don't live as a lion, even for a minute, far from it: you live like something far lower than a sheep for years and years and know that you have to live like that.'[37]

Benjamin and Gramsci were victims of fascism. But in the post-war epoch, too, the note struck within Western Marxism was often no less sombre. Perhaps the most powerful single essay by Althusser, for example, could describe the social development from birth to childhood that initiates the unconscious, with fierce violence, as an ordeal 'all adult men have passed: they are the *never forgetful* witnesses, and very often the victims, of this victory, bearing in their most hidden, i.e. in their most clamorous parts, the wounds, weaknesses and stiffnesses that

[36] *Illuminations*, pp. 259–60, 257.
[37] *Prison Notebooks*, p. XCIII.

result from this struggle for human life or death. Some, the majority, have emerged more or less unscathed – or at least, give this out to be the case; many of these veterans bear the marks throughout their lives; some will die from their fight, though at some remove, the old wounds suddenly opening again in psychotic explosion, in madness, the ultimate compulsion of a "negative therapeutic reaction"; others, more numerous, as "normally" as you like, in the guise of an "organic" decay. Humanity only inscribes its official deaths on its war memorials: those who were able to die on time, i.e. late, as men, in human wars in which only *human* wolves and gods tear and sacrifice one another.'[38] Yet another savage metaphor was to be used by Sartre, to describe the relations between men in a universe of scarcity: 'Our fellow appears to us as a counter-man in so far as he who is the same appears as radically other – that is to say, bearer of a threat of death to us. In other words, by and large we understand his ends (they are our own), his means (we share the same), the dialectical structure of his acts; but we understand them as if they were the traits of *another species*, our demoniac double. No being, in effect – neither wild beasts nor microbes – is so deadly for man as an intelligent, carnivorous, cruel species capable of understanding and foiling human intelligence, whose end is precisely the destruction of man. This species is, of course, our own, as each man apprehends it in every other in the milieu of scarcity.'[39] Passages like these belong to a literature fundamentally foreign to the world of Marx, Labriola, or Lenin. They betray a subterranean pessimism, beyond the declared intentions or theses of their authors[40] – none of

[38] *Lenin and Philosophy*, pp. 189–90.

[39] *Critique de la Raison Dialectique*, p. 208.

[40] At this point, it is necessary to say something of the writings of Sebastiano Timpanaro, alluded to earlier. Timpanaro's work contains the most coherent and eloquent rejection of what he himself calls 'Western Marxism' to have been written since the war. It is, therefore, all the more striking that in a number of critical respects his own work conforms, despite itself, to the pattern considered above. For Timpanaro's work too is essentially philosophical – not political or economic – in focus. Moreover, it too makes a central appeal to an intellectual ancestor prior to Marx, through whom Marxism is then substantially reinterpreted. In this case, the commanding predecessor is the poet Giacomo Leopardi, whose particular form of materialism is deemed the salutary and necessary complement to that of Marx and Engels, because of its unflinching awareness of the insurmountable limits – of frailty and mortality – imposed on man by a hostile nature. The most distinctive theme of Timpanaro's own work is therefore the in-

whom renounced optimism of volition in the struggle against fascism or capitalism. Marxism spoke thoughts once unthinkable for socialism through them.

The circle of traits defining Western Marxism as a distinct tradition can now be summarized. Born from the failure of proletarian revolutions in the advanced zones of European capitalism after the First World War, it developed within an ever increasing scission between socialist theory and working-class practice. The gulf between the two, originally opened up by the imperialist isolation of the Soviet State, was institutionally widened and fixed by the bureaucratization of the USSR and of the Comintern under Stalin. To the exponents of the new Marxism that emerged in the West, the official Communist movement represented the sole real embodiment of the international working class with meaning for them – whether they joined it, allied with it or rejected it. The structural divorce of theory and practice inherent in the nature of the Communist Parties of this epoch precluded unitary politico-intellectual work of the type that defined classical Marxism. The result was a seclusion of theorists in universities,

---

evitability of the ultimate victory, not of man over history, but of nature over man. It is thus more finally pessimistic, with a classical sadness, than that of perhaps any other socialist thinker of this century. In all these ways, Timpanaro can be regarded as paradoxically yet unmistakably part of the tradition of Western Marxism that he opposes. It could be argued that the notable importance of ancient philology – a discipline entirely dominated by non-Marxist scholarship, from Wilamowitz to Pasquali – in his formation also corresponds to the pattern discerned in this essay. This said, it must immediately be emphasized that in other respects Timpanaro's work presents a genuine and manifest contrast with the norms of Western Marxism. The differences are that Timpanaro's philosophy has never been primarily reduced to a concern with epistemology, but has sought to develop a substantive outlook on the world, in a critical allegiance to the heritage of Engels; that his use of Leopardi has never relied on a claim that Marx was ever influenced by or knew of the poet, or that the two systems of thought are at all homogeneous – Leopardi being presented as supplying something missing, not something hidden, in Marx; and that his pessimism is consciously declared and defended as such, in a limpid prose. Lastly, it may be said that these traits have been accompanied by a degree of freedom from the field of force of official Communism greater than that of any other figure of Western Marxism. Timpanaro born in 1923, was uniquely neither a member of the Communist Party nor an unattached intellectual, but a militant in another working-class party – first on the left of the PSI (Italian Socialist Party) and then of the PSIUP, in Italy.

far from the life of the proletariat in their own countries, and a contraction of theory from economics and politics into philosophy. This specialization was accompanied by an increasing difficulty of language, whose technical barriers were a function of its distance from the masses. It was also conversely attended by a decreasing level of international knowledge or communication between theorists themselves from different countries. The loss of any dynamic contact with working-class practice in turn displaced Marxist theory towards contemporary non-Marxist and idealist systems of thought, with which it now typically developed in close if contradictory symbiosis. At the same time, the concentration of theorists into professional philosophy, together with the discovery of Marx's own early writings, led to a general retrospective search for intellectual ancestries to Marxism in anterior European philosophical thought, and a reinterpretation of historical materialism itself in the light of them. The results of this pattern were three-fold. Firstly, there was a marked predominance of epistemological work, focused essentially on problems of method. Secondly, the major substantive field in which method was actually applied became aesthetics – or cultural superstructures in a broader sense. Finally the main theoretical departures outside this field, which developed new themes absent from classical Marxism – mostly in a speculative manner – revealed a consistent pessimism. Method as impotence, art as consolation, pessimism as quiescence: it is not difficult to perceive elements of all these in the complexion of Western Marxism. For the root determinant of this tradition was its formation by defeat – the long decades of set-back and stagnation, many of them terrible ones in any historical perspective, undergone by the Western working class after 1920.

But nor can the tradition as a whole be reduced to this. Despite everything, its major thinkers remained immune to reformism.[41] For all their distance from the masses, none capitulated to triumphant capitalism as Second International theorists like Kautsky, far closer to class struggle, had done before them. Moreover, the historical experience which their work articulated, amidst its very inhibitions and aphasias, was also in certain critical respects the most *advanced* in the

---

[41] Horkheimer is the only example of renegacy: but he was always intellectually of secondary rank as a thinker within the Frankfurt School.

world – encompassing the highest forms of the capitalist economy, the oldest industrial proletariats, and the longest intellectual traditions of socialism. Something of the wealth and complexity of this total record, as well as its misery and failure, inevitably entered into the Marxism that it produced or permitted – if always in oblique and incomplete forms. In its own chosen fields, this Marxism achieved a sophistication greater than that of any previous phase of historical materialism. Its depth in these was bought at the price of the width of its range. But if there was a drastic narrowing of focus, there was no complete paralysis of energy. Today, the full experience of the past fifty years of imperialism remains a central and unavoidable sum still to be reckoned up by the workers' movement. Western Marxism has been an integral part of that history, and no new generation of revolutionary socialists in the imperialist countries can simply ignore or bypass it. To settle accounts with this tradition – both learning and breaking from it – is thus one of the preconditions of a local renewal of Marxist theory today. This necessary double movement of reconnaissance and rupture is not, of course, an exclusive task. The nature of its object precludes this. For in the last resort, the very ties of this tradition to a particular geography have also been its dependence and weakness. Marxism aspires in principle to be a *universal* science – no more amenable to merely national or continental ascriptions than any other objective cognition of reality. In this sense, the term 'Western' inevitably implies a *limiting* judgement. Lack of universality is an index of deficiency of truth. Western Marxism was necessarily less than Marxism to the extent that it was Western. Historical materialism can exercise its full powers only when it is free from parochialism, of any kind. It has yet to recover them.

5
Contrasts and Conclusions

The advent of a new period in the workers' movement, bringing to an end the long class pause that divided theory from practice, is now however visible. The French Revolt of May 1968 marked in this respect a profound historical turning-point. For the first time in nearly 50 years, a massive revolutionary upsurge occurred within advanced capitalism – in time of peace, under conditions of imperialist prosperity and bourgeois democracy. The onset of this explosion bypassed the French Communist Party. With this, the two crucial conditions of the historic non-coincidence of theory and politics in Western Europe for the first time started to fall. The re-emergence of revolutionary masses outside the control of a bureaucratized party rendered *potentially* conceivable the unification of Marxist theory and working-class practice once again. In the event, of course, the May Revolt was not a revolution; and the main force of the proletariat in France has neither organizationally nor ideologically abandoned the PCF. The distance between revolutionary theory and mass struggle was far from abolished overnight in Paris during May–June 1968; but it closed to its narrowest gap in Europe since the general strike was defeated in Turin during the turmoil of 1920. The revolt in France, moreover, was not to remain an isolated experience. The subsequent years have seen a widening international wave of working-class insurgency in the imperialist world, unlike anything since the early twenties. In 1969, the Italian proletariat unleashed the greatest wave of strikes ever recorded in the country; in 1972 the British working class launched the most successful industrial offensive in its history, paralysing the national economy; in 1973 Japanese labour mounted its largest assault against capital to date. In 1974, the world capitalist economy entered its first major synchronized recession since the war. The chance of a revolutionary circuit reopening between Marxist theory and mass practice, looped through real struggles of the industrial working class, has become steadily greater. The consequences of such a reunification of theory and practice would be to transform Marxism itself – recreating conditions which, in their time, produced the founders of historical materialism.

Meanwhile, the series of upheavals inaugurated by the May Revolt has had another, critical impact on the contemporary prospects of historical materialism in the advanced capitalist zone. Western Marxism, from Lukács and Korsch to Gramsci or Althusser, occupied in many respects the front of the stage in the whole intellectual history of the European Left, after the victory of Stalin in the USSR. But throughout this period, another tradition of an entirely different character subsisted and developed 'off-stage' – for the first time to gain wider political attention during and after the French explosion. This was, of course, the theory and legacy of Trotsky. Western Marxism, as we have seen, was always magnetically polarized towards official Communism as the only historical incarnation of the international proletariat as a revolutionary class. It never completely accepted Stalinism; yet it never actively combated it either. But whatever nuance of attitude successive thinkers adopted towards it, for all of them there was no other effective reality or milieu of socialist action outside it. It was this that divided it from Trotsky's work by a political universe. For Trotsky's life from the death of Lenin onwards was devoted to a practical and theoretical struggle to free the international workers' movement from bureaucratic domination so that it could resume a successful overthrow of capitalism on a world scale. Defeated in the inner-party conflict within the CPSU in the twenties, and exiled from the USSR as a standing danger to the regime symbolized by Stalin, Trotsky's most enduring development of Marxist theory began in exile.[1] His new work was born from the matrix of a tremendous mass upheaval – the October Revolution. But Trotskyism as a system was a delayed birth: it largely post-dated the Revolution, when the experience that made it possible had already

[1] Although, of course, it had its prophetic origins in his pre-revolutionary work *Results and Prospects*.

disappeared. Thus Trotsky's first major production in exile was – uniquely for a Marxist theorist of his stature – a work of concrete *history*. His *History of the Russian Revolution* (1930) remains in many ways the most commanding example of Marxist historical literature to this day; and the only one where the skill and passion of a historian were joined to the activity and memory of a political leader and organizer, in a major reconstruction of the past.

Trotsky's next achievement was in some ways even more significant. Isolated on a Turkish island, he wrote from a distance a sequence of texts on the rise of Nazism in Germany, whose quality as concrete studies of a *political conjuncture* is unmatched in the records of historical materialism. In this field, Lenin himself never produced any work of comparable depth and complexity. Trotsky's writings on German Fascism constitute, in fact, the first real Marxist analysis of a twentieth century *capitalist State* – the making of the Nazi dictatorship.[1] The internationalist nature of his intervention, designed to arm the German working class against the mortal danger threatening it, was maintained throughout the rest of his life. Exiled and hunted from country to country, without physical contact with the proletariat of any nation, he continued to produce political analyses of the highest order of the West European scene. France, England and Spain were all examined by him with a mastery of the national specificity of their social formations that Lenin – overwhelmingly concentrated on Russia – had never attained.[2] Finally, he initiated a rigorous and comprehensive theory of the nature of the Soviet State and the fate of the USSR under Stalin, documented and developed with a classical control of evidence.[3] The historical scale of Trotsky's accomplishment is still difficult to realize today.

[1] This judgement may seem paradoxical: we shall return to it elsewhere. It is symptomatic of the fate of Trotsky's legacy that these texts on Germany should not have been published in book form until 1970 – when the first German edition appeared. For an English translation of this, see now *The Struggle Against Fascism in Germany*, New York 1971.

[2] Now collected respectively in *Whither France?* (1970), *On Britain* (1973), and *The Spanish Revolution* (1973), all published in New York. The writings on Britain mostly date from the twenties; but the collection above omits some important texts of the thirties.

[3] Above all, *The Revolution Betrayed*; *The Class Nature of the Soviet State*; and *In Defense of Marxism* (New York 1965).

There is no space here to unravel the subsequent legacy of Trotsky's thought and work. One day, this other tradition – persecuted, reviled, isolated, divided – will have to be studied in all the diversity of its underground channels and streams. It may surprise future historians with its resources. Here it is only necessary to comment on the work of two or three of the later heirs of Trotsky. The most gifted members of the next generation after him were both from the East European intelligentsia, on the borderlands between Poland and Russia. Isaac Deutscher (1907–67), born near Cracow, was a militant in the illegal Polish Communist Party, who broke with the Comintern over its policy towards the ascent of Nazism in 1933, and fought for five years in an oppositional Trotskyist group within the working class in Pilsudski's Poland. On the eve of the Second World War, he rejected Trotsky's decision to organize a Fourth International, renouncing the attempt to maintain a political unity of theory and practice that he now believed to be impossible, and emigrated to England.[5] There, after the War, he became a professional historian, producing the major series of works on the course and outcome of the Soviet Revolution for which he became famous throughout the world. Despite his divergences from Trotsky, the continuity of focus between them could scarcely have been closer. Trotsky was working on a life of Stalin when he died; Deutscher's first work was a biography of Stalin, taking up where his predecessor had left off. Thereafter Deutscher's greatest work was to be a biography of Trotsky himself.[6] His most important contemporary and colleague was another historian. Roman Rosdolsky (1898–1967), born in Lvov, was one of the founders of the Communist Party of the Western Ukraine. Working under the direction of Ryazanov as a corresponding member of the Marx-Engels Institute in Vienna, he rallied to Trotsky's critique of the consolidation of Stalinism in the USSR and of Comintern policy towards fascism in Germany in the early thirties. From 1934 to 1938, he returned to Lvov and worked in the local Trotskyist movement in Galicia, while also writing a long

---

[5] For Deutscher's early career, see Daniel Singer, 'Armed with a Pen', in D. Horowitz (ed.), *Isaac Deutscher, The Man and His Work*, London 1971, pp. 20–37.

[6] *The Prophet Armed* (1954); *The Prophet Unarmed* (1959); *The Prophet Outcast* (1963).

study of the history of serfdom in the region. Captured by the German Army during the Second World War, he was imprisoned in Nazi concentration camps. On his release in 1945, he emigrated to the United States, where he worked as an isolated researcher in New York and Detroit, abandoning direct political activity. There he wrote one of the few significant Marxist texts on the national problem in Europe to appear since the time of Lenin.[7] His *magnum opus*, however, was a long, two-volume examination of Marx's *Grundrisse* and its relation to *Capital* – published posthumously in West Germany in 1968.[8] The aim of this major reconstruction of the architecture of Marx's mature economic thought was to make it possible for contemporary Marxism to rejoin the central tradition of economic theory within historical materialism, broken off with the expiry of Austro-Marxism in the inter-war period. Trotsky himself had written no major economic work, unlike most theorists of his generation: Rosdolsky himself, not an economist by training, undertook his work out of a sense of duty to succeeding generations, as a lone survivor of the East European culture that had once produced Bolshevism and Austro-Marxism.[9] His hope was not in vain. Four years later, Ernest Mandel – a Belgian Trotskyist, who had been active in the Resistance and imprisoned by the Nazis, before becoming prominent in the Fourth International after the War – published in Germany a full-scale study of *Late Capitalism*, directly indebted to Rosdolsky:[10] the first theoretical analysis of the global development of the capitalist mode of production since the Second World War, conceived within the framework of classical Marxist categories.

[7] *Friedrich Engels und das Problem der 'Geschichtslosen Völker'*, Hanover 1964. For Rosdolsky's biography, see the notice in *Quatrième Internationale*, No. 33, April 1968.

[8] *Zur Entstehungsgeschichte des Marxschen Kapitals*, Frankfurt 1968.

[9] 'The author is neither an economist nor a philosopher by profession. He would not have ventured to write a commentary on the *Grundrisse*, if there had existed today a school of Marxist theorists better equipped for this task – as there did in the first third of this century. But the last generation of renowned Marxist thinkers for the most part fell victims to the terror of Hitler or of Stalin.' *Zur Entstehungsgeschichte*, pp. 10–11.

[10] *Der Spätkapitalismus (Versuch einer Erklärung)*, Frankfurt 1972; dedication to Rosdolsky, p. 9. [The enlarged English edition, London NLB 1975, omits the subtitle of the German edition.]

The tradition descended from Trotsky has thus been a polar contrast, in most essential respects, to that of Western Marxism. It concentrated on politics and economics, not philosophy. It was resolutely internationalist, never confined in concern or horizon to a single culture or country. It spoke a language of clarity and urgency, whose finest prose (Trotsky or Deutscher) yet possessed a literary quality equal or superior to that of any other tradition. It filled no chairs in universities. Its members were hunted and outlawed. Trotsky was killed in Mexico. Deutscher and Rosdolsky were exiles, unable to return to Poland or the Ukraine. Mandel is proscribed from France, West Germany and the United States to this day. Other names could be added. The price paid for the attempt to maintain a Marxist unity of theory and practice, even in cases where it was eventually renounced, was a high one. But the gain made, for the future of socialism, was in exchange an immense one. Today, this politico-theoretical heritage provides one of the central elements for any renaissance of revolutionary Marxism on an international scale. The acquisitions it embodies have their own limits and frailties. Trotsky's development of the particular formula of the Russian Revolution into a general rule for the underdeveloped world remains problematic; his writings on France and Spain are not of the same sureness as those on Germany; his judgement on the Second World War, a departure from his analysis of Nazism, was mistaken. Deutscher's optimism about the prospects for internal reform within the USSR after Stalin was unfounded. Rosdolsky's main labours were expository, rather than exploratory, in scope. Mandel's study, coming after so long a silence in its field, was subtitled deliberately an 'Attempt at Explanation'. In general, the progress of Marxist theory could not vault over the material conditions of its own production – the social practice of the real proletariat of the time. The combination of enforced isolation from the main detachments of the organized working class throughout the world, and protracted absence of revolutionary mass upsurges in the central lands of industrial capitalism, inevitably left its effects on the Trotskyist tradition as a whole. It, too, was subject to the ultimate dictates of the long epoch of historical defeat for the working class in the West. Its defiance of the turn of the time, which set it apart from Western Marxism, exacted its particular penalties. Reaffirmation of the validity and reality of socialist revolution and proletarian democracy, against so many events which denied them, involuntarily inclined this tradition towards conservatism. The preservation of classical doctrines took priority over their development. Triumphalism in the cause of the working class, and catastrophism in the analysis of capitalism, asserted more by will than by intellect, were to be the typical vices of this tradition in its routine forms. It will be necessary to make a historical inventory of the achievements and failures of this experience. A systematic critical assessment of the legacy of Trotsky and his successors, comparable to that which is now potentially available for the heritage of Western Marxism, is overdue. At the same time, the growth of international class struggles since the late sixties has for the first time since the defeat of the Left Opposition in Russia, started to create an objective possibility of the reappearance of the political ideas associated with Trotsky in central areas of working-class debate and activity. When and as this junction occurs, their values will be assayed in the wider criticism of mass proletarian practice.

Meanwhile, the change of temperature since the end of the sixties has also had its effects on Western Marxism. The eventual reunification of theory and practice in a mass revolutionary movement, free of bureaucratic trammels, would mean the end of this tradition. As a historical form, it will fall into extinction when the divorce which produced it is overcome. The preliminary signs of this supersession are visible today: but it is by no means yet an accomplished process. The present period is still one of transition. The large Communist Parties of the European continent, which always remained the underlying gravitational field of Western Marxism, have far from disappeared; their dominance within their national working classes has not notably diminished, although their credit as revolutionary organizations has been weakened among the intelligentsia. Many of the major theorists of Western Marxism discussed above are now dead. Those who survive have so far proved unable to respond to the new conjuncture created since the May upheaval in France, with any notable development of their theory. For the most part, their intellectual course has probably already been run. Among a younger generation, formed under the influence of this tradition, there has been a certain shift towards a closer concern with economic and political theory, beyond the philosophical perimeter of their elders.[11] This shift, however, has often been accompanied by a simple displacement of referential horizon from Soviet to Chinese Communism. Organizationally and ideologically vaguer as a pole of orientation, the substitution of China for the USSR has otherwise basically preserved the tacit political heteronomy of Western Marxism. The passage of some of the older generation of theorists – Althusser or Sartre – more or less directly from one to the other merely confirms the continuity of the structural relationship.[12] Fundamentally new departures within Western Marxism must be regarded as imponderable, so long as it obtains. The senior theorists of this tradition who are left may in any case now be confined to philosophical repetition and exhaustion. The future of their pupils is naturally more open.

Whatever its fate in its original zone of implantation, meanwhile, the last few years have seen the introduction of the Western Marxism produced in Germany, France and Italy on a wide scale in new regions of the capitalist world – above all, the Anglo-Saxon and Nordic countries. The consequences of this diffusion are unforeseeable. None of these nations has historically possessed a strong Communist movement; and none has hitherto generated any major body of Marxist theory. Some have specific assets of their own, however. In England, especially, the working class has remained industrially one of the most powerful in the world, and the calibre of Marxist *historiography* has probably been superior to that of any other country. The relative modesty to date of Marxist culture in a wider sense in this region, may itself be subject to surprisingly swift changes. For the law of uneven development governs the tempo and distribution of theory too: it can transform laggard into leading countries, benefiting from the advantages of latecomers, in a comparatively short period. At any rate, it can be said with some confidence that *until* it has mastered the terrain of the United States and England – respectively the lands of the wealthiest imperialist class and of the oldest working class in the world

---

[11] The most notable works of this type are those of Nicos Poulantzas: English translations, *Political Power and Social Classes* (London NLB/SW 1973) and *Fascism and Dictatorship* (London NLB 1974).

[12] The nature and influence of Maoism fall outside the scope of this essay: discussion of it at length will be necessary elsewhere.

– Marxism will not have measured itself against the full reach of the problems with which the civilization of capital confronts it, in the second half of the twentieth century. The failure of the Third International, even in the heyday of Lenin, to make any serious headway in the Anglo-Saxon powers, when the USA and Britain were the two greatest centres of world capitalism, indicates the degree of *incompletion* of historical materialism at the very height of its accomplishments as a living revolutionary theory. Today, the formidable scientific problems posed to the socialist movement by the capitalist mode of production at its *strongest*, rather than at its weakest, still largely remain to be solved. Marxism in this sense has yet to acquit itself of its most difficult tasks. It is unlikely to square up to these until it is finally at home in the mature imperial bastions of the Anglo-Saxon world.

For after the prolonged, winding detour of Western Marxism, the questions left unanswered by Lenin's generation, and made impossible to answer by the rupture of theory and practice in Stalin's epoch, continue to await replies. They do not lie within the jurisdiction of philosophy. They concern the central economic and political realities that have dominated world history in the last fifty years. There is no space here to do more than provide the briefest list of them. First and foremost, what is the real nature and structure of *bourgeois democracy* as a type of State system, that has become the normal mode of capitalist power in the advanced countries? What type of *revolutionary strategy* is capable of overthrowing this historical form of State – so distinct from that of Tsarist Russia? What would be the institutional forms of *socialist democracy* in the West, beyond it? Marxist theory has scarcely touched these three subjects, in their inter-connection. What is the meaning and position of the *nation* as a social unit, in a world divided by classes? Above all, what are the complex mechanisms of *nationalism*, as a mass phenomenon of elemental force in the last two centuries? Neither of these problems has ever received an adequate response, from the time of Marx and Engels onwards. What are the *contemporary laws of motion of capitalism* as a mode of production; and are there new forms of *crisis* specific to them? What is the true configuration of *imperialism* as an international system of economic and political domination? Work has only just begun again on these issues, in a landscape long changed since Lenin or Bauer. Finally what are the basic characteristics and dynamics of the *bureaucratic States* that have emerged from the socialist revolutions in the backward countries, in both their *unity* and *distinction* from each other? How was it possible for *the destruction of proletarian democracy* after the revolution in Russia to be followed by the making of revolutions *without proletarian democracy from the outset* in China and elsewhere: and what are the determinate limits to such a process? Trotsky inaugurated analysis of the former; he did not live to see the latter. It is these serried questions that constitute the central challenge to historical materialism today.

The precondition of their solution is, as we have seen, the rise of a mass revolutionary movement, free of organizational constraint, in the homelands of industrial capitalism. Only then will a new unity of socialist theory and working-class practice be possible, capable of endowing Marxism with the powers necessary to produce the knowledge it lacks today. The forms in which this theory of the future will emerge cannot be foreseen, nor its bearers. It would be a mistake to assume that they will necessarily repeat the classical models of the past. Virtually all the major theorists of historical materialism to date, from Marx or Engels themselves to the Bolsheviks, from the leading figures of Austro-Marxism to those of Western Marxism, have been intellectuals drawn from the possessing classes: more often than not, of higher rather than lower bourgeois origin.[18] Gramsci is the sole example to have come from a background of actual poverty; but even he was born far from the proletariat. It is impossible not to see in this pattern a provisional immaturity of the international working class as a whole, in a world-historical perspective. It is enough to think of the consequences for the October Revolution of the fragility of the Bolshevik Old Guard, a political leadership recruited overwhelmingly from the Russian intelligentsia, superimposed on a still largely uneducated working class: the ease with which both Old Guard and proletarian vanguard were eliminated by Stalin in the twenties was not unconnected

---

[18] The conventional appellation 'petty-bourgeois intellectual', is not appropriate for most of the figures discussed above. Many of them came from families of wealthy manufacturers, merchants and bankers (Engels, Luxemburg, Bauer, Lukács, Grossmann, Adorno, Benjamin, Marcuse, Sweezy); large landowners (Plekhanov, Mehring, Labriola); senior lawyers or bureaucrats (Marx, Lenin).

with the social gap between them. A working-class movement capable of achieving a durable self-emancipation will not reproduce this dualism. The 'organic intellectuals' envisaged by Gramsci, generated within the ranks of the proletariat itself, have not yet occupied the structural role in revolutionary socialism that he believed would be theirs.[14] The extreme forms of esotericism that have characterized Western Marxism were symptomatic of 'traditional intellectuals' in Gramsci's sense, in a period when there was little or no contact between socialist theory and proletarian practice. But in the long run, the future of Marxist theory will lie with intellectuals organically produced by the industrial working classes of the imperialist world themselves, as they steadily gain in cultural skill and self-confidence.

The final word can rest with Lenin. His famous dictum that 'without revolutionary theory, there can be no revolutionary movement', is often and rightly quoted. But he also wrote, with equal weight: 'Correct revolutionary theory . . . assumes final shape only in close connection with the practical activity of a truly mass and truly revolutionary movement.'[15] Every clause here counts. Revolutionary theory can be undertaken in relative isolation – Marx in the British Museum, Lenin in war-bound Zurich: but it can only acquire a *correct* and *final* form when bound to the collective struggles of the working class itself. Mere formal membership of a party organization, of the type familiar in recent history, does not suffice to provide such a bond: a *close connection* with the *practical activity* of the proletariat is necessary. Nor is militancy in a small revolutionary group enough: there must be a linkage with *actual masses*. Conversely, linkage with a mass movement is not enough either, for the latter may be reformist: it is only when the masses are *themselves revolutionary*, that theory can complete

---

[14] Perhaps the most distinguished socialist thinker to have so far come from the ranks of the Western working class itself has been a Briton, Raymond Williams. Yet Williams's work, while it has corresponded closely to the pattern of Western Marxism in its typically aesthetic and cultural focus, has not been that of a Marxist. However, its class history – steadily and confidently present throughout Williams's writings – has conferred on this work certain qualities which cannot be found anywhere else in contemporary socialist writing, and which will be part of any future revolutionary culture.

[15] 'Left-Wing Communism: An Infantile Disorder', *Selected Works*, Vol. III. p. 378.

its eminent vocation. These five conditions for the successful pursuit of Marxism have not been assembled anywhere in the advanced capitalist world since the Second World War. The prospects for their reappearance are now, however, at last increasing. When a truly revolutionary movement is born in a mature working class, the 'final shape' of theory will have no exact precedent. All that can be said is that when the masses themselves speak, theoreticians – of the sort the West has produced for fifty years – will necessarily be silent.

Afterword

The claims with which the essay above concludes must inspire certain reservations today. For these lack some indispensable qualifications and distinctions, without which their logic is ultimately a reductionist one. Their apocalyptic tone is itself a suspect sign, of difficulties peremptorily evaded or ignored. To explore these difficulties adequately – not to speak of solving them – would need another essay. The most that can be done here is merely to indicate the central weakness in the construction of the preceding text. This can be stated succinctly. Marxist theory – it is argued throughout,' in accentuated terms towards the end – acquires its proper contours only in direct relation to a mass revolutionary movement. When the latter is effectively absent or defeated, the former is inevitably deformed or eclipsed. The premise of this pervasive theme is, of course, the tenet of the 'unity of theory and practice' traditionally deemed to define Marxist epistemology as such. There are certain hints in the essay that the relation between the two is more complex than has customarily been conceded; but as a whole, the text is a sustained affirmation of the fundamental bond between science and class, historical materialism and proletarian insurgency, in this century. The actual conditions or precise horizons of the unity of theory and practice postulated are nowhere examined. The result is that the conclusions of the essay invite an 'activist' reading of its theses that could be scientifically untenable and politically irresponsible.

For there is an insuperable objection to any account of Marxism such as that suggested in the last pages of this essay. It is strange that it has not been made more frequently before. If the proper designation for Marxism is historical materialism, it must be – above all – a theory of history. Yet history is – pre-eminently – the *past*. The present and the future are also, of course, historical, and it is to these that the traditional precepts on the role of practice within Marxism involuntarily refer. But the past cannot be altered by any practice of the present. Its events will always be reinterpreted, its epochs rediscovered, by later generations: they cannot, in any sober materialist sense, be changed. Politically, the fate of living men and women – in the actual present and the foreseeable future – is immeasurably more important for a socialist than any other consideration. Scientifically, however, the over-whelmingly preponderant domain of ascertainable knowledge is the realm of the dead. The past, which cannot be amended or undone, can be known with greater certainty than the present, whose actions have yet to be done; and there is more of it. There will thus always remain an inherent scissiparity between knowledge and action, theory and practice, for any possible science of history. No responsible Marxism can either abdicate from the task of comprehending the immense universe of the past, or claim to exercise the jurisdiction of a material transformation of it. Marxist theory is thus not, despite every laudable temptation, to be equated with a revolutionary sociology. It can never be reduced to the 'analysis of the current conjuncture', in a now fashionable terminology. For by definition, what is current soon passes. To confine Marxism to the contemporary is to condemn it to a perpetual oblivion, in which the present ceases to be knowable once it recedes into the past.[1] Few socialists would dissent from this. Yet the

---

[1] This is not an imaginary doctrine. A recent work declares: 'Marxism, as a theoretical and political practice, gains nothing from its association with historical writing and historical research. The study of history is not only scientifically but also politically valueless. The object of history, the past, no matter how it is conceived, cannot affect present conditions. Historical events do not exist and can have no material effectivity in the present. The conditions of existence of present social relations necessarily exist in and are constantly reproduced in the present. It is not the "present", what the past has vouchsafed to allow us, but the "current situation" which it is the object of Marxist theory to elucidate and of Marxist political practice to act upon. All Marxist theory, however abstract it may be, however general its field of application, exists to make possible the analysis of the current situation. ... A historical analysis of the "current situation" is impos-sible.' B. Hindness and P. Hirst, *Pre-Capitalist Modes of Production*, London 1975, p. 312. The authors of this pronouncement, remote descendants of Althusser, have the distinction of proclaiming with some precision the exasperated consequences of a logic whose initial premises may often appear casual and uncontroversial, in

exact statute of history within historical materialism has paradoxically never hitherto been adequately debated. It is incompatible with any philosophical pragmatism. Marxism has in this sense perhaps yet to take with all due seriousness its claim to be a 'science of history'. For the proud title of historical materialism can only be earned by a modest respect for the reality of its two terms. This respect necessitates a limit to the notion of the unity of theory and practice. The great political problems before the international working class in the twentieth century, whose absence from the tradition of Western Marxism has been emphasized here, certainly remain subject to its regulation. But the exact forms and shifts of its rule have never yet been properly studied. Yet a renunciation of the general and uncritical universality they have often ascribed to the union of theory and practice, may actually aid Marxists to focus more precisely on the particular social conditions for the emergence of revolutionary theory, and the specific scientific protocols for its validation.

This is not say that two separate and sealed domains should be distinguished within historical materialism – an active 'politics' and a passive 'history', the one entirely governed by the tidal practices of the masses, the other ideally exempt from them. But it is to pose the question, hitherto unduly neglected, of the relationship – actual and potential – between 'historiography' and 'theory' within Marxist culture as a whole. The political determinations of modern writing of history, whether Marxist or non-Marxist, are so well known that they need little reassertion here. (They do not, of course, constitute a form of the unity between theory and practice in the classical sense.) The historical acquisitions available or necessary for modern writing in political or economic theory, within Marxism, have not been so often considered. It should, in fact, be evident that advances within Marxist historiography are potentially of critical importance for the development of Marxist theory. Yet, despite the formation of major schools of Marxist historiography in nearly all the advanced capitalist countries, it cannot be said that historical materialism as a theoretical system has benefited commensurately. There has been comparatively little integration of the findings of Marxist history into Marxist politics or

conventional Marxist accounts of the unity of theory and practice within historical materialism.

economics, to date. This anomaly appears all the greater when it is recollected that no professional historiography of this type existed in the epoch of classical Marxism; while its advent in a later epoch has not had many noticeable effects within post-classical Marxism. Because of its novelty, the nature of its import for the structure of historical materialism as a whole has thus yet to be seen. At the least, it might be surmised that the balance between 'history' and 'theory' may be redressed in any Marxist culture of the future, altering its present configuration.

There is another emphasis in this essay which needs a related modification. The emblem of the unity of theory and practice is used to develop a structural contrast between classical and 'Western' Marxism. This contrast is certainly not a false one. Yet the manner of its presentation here tends to exempt classical Marxism unduly from critical scrutiny. The latter's practical unity with the struggles of the working class of its time, which genuinely renders it so much superior to the tradition which succeeded it, appears as a standard of absolute comparison within historical materialism. Once, however, the rule of the unity of theory with practice is relativized, even the science that was most closely and heroically linked to the working class must be subject to a constant and scrupulous reassessment. If the essay does not ascribe any perfection to classical Marxism, the limits to which it refers are nevertheless presented essentially as incompletions – in effect, lacunae whose remedy was a further development of the theory, which Western Marxism was later unable to achieve. The possibility that there may have been elements in the classical heritage which were not so much incomplete as incorrect is not taken with sufficient seriousness. It is in part precisely the accumulation of historical knowledge about the past that was unavailable to the first generations of Marxists as they lived through it as their present, which permits and enjoins new scientific interrogation of their work today.

In other words, classical Marxism should be submitted to the same rigorous scrutiny and critical appraisal as the post-classical tradition that derived from it. The courage and calm needed for such a programme would be much greater than in the case of Western Marxism, given the veneration with which nearly all serious socialists have treated the classical masters of historical materialism, and the absence to date of any intellectual critique of these that remained equally and resolutely revolutionary in political position. The greatest respect is, however, compatible with the greatest lucidity. The study of classical Marxism today needs a combination of scholarly knowledge and sceptical honesty that it has not yet received. In the post-war epoch, the best and most original work in this field has usually taken the form of ingenious reinterpretations of one canonical text or author, Marx or Engels or Lenin, to refute conventional notions about another, often with the aim of combating bourgeois criticisms or misinterpretations of Marxism as such. Today, it is necessary to abandon this practice, and to proceed instead to scrutinize the credentials of the texts of classical Marxism themselves, without any prior assumption of their necessary coherence or correctness. In fact, the most important responsibility for contemporary socialists may be to isolate the main theoretical weaknesses of classical Marxism, to explain the historical reasons for these, and to remedy them. The presence of errors is one of the marks of any science: the pretence of their absence has merely discredited the claim of historical materialism to be one. The customary comparison of Marx with Copernicus or Galileo, if it is to be made, should be taken seriously: no one imagines today that the writings of the latter are free from critical mistakes and contradictions. Their very status as pioneers of modern astronomy or physics is the guarantee of the inevitability of their errors, at the dawn of the development of a new science. The same must be true *a priori* of Marxism. The central problems that are posed by the classical texts of this tradition obviously cannot be explored here. However, merely to assert the formal necessity of doing so, without any specification, would be little more than a token piety. In conclusion, therefore, certain critical areas where the heritage of classical Marxism appears inadequate or unsatisfactory, may be suggested. The fleeting comments to be made on them naturally do not pretend to a proper treatment of the issues concerned. They are merely a few rapid semaphores of problems to be considered elsewhere. For purposes of convenience, they will be confined to the work of the outstanding trio of the classical tradition – Marx, Lenin and Trotsky.

The greatness of Marx's overall achievement needs no reiteration here. Indeed it was the very range of his general vision of the future which in a certain sense induced the local illusions and myopias in his scanning of the present of his own time. Marx could not remain so politically and theoretically central to the later twentieth century, if he had not at times been out of synchrony with the later nineteenth century in which he lived. His mistakes and omissions may be said to have typically been the price of his foresights. It is the sum of scientific knowledge now available about the history of capitalism – so much greater than that at his disposal – which should permit historical materialism today to surpass them. It is in this respect that there are three areas where Marx's work appears centrally uncertain, from a contemporary perspective.

(i) The first of these is his treatment of the capitalist State. His early writings started to theorize, in effect, the structures of what was later to be bourgeois democracy, before it existed anywhere in Europe – but at a very abstract and philosophical level. Then in 1848–50 he wrote a concrete, historical study of the peculiar dictatorial state created by Napoleon III in France – his only such venture. Thereafter, he never directly analysed the English parliamentary state under which he lived for the rest of his life. If anything, he tended to generalize 'Bonapartism' abusively as the typical form of the modern bourgeois state, because of his political memories of its counter-revolutionary role in 1848. He was consequently unable to analyse the Third Republic in France, when it emerged after the defeat of 1870. Finally, because of his preoccupation with 'militarist' Bonapartism, he seems by contrast to have tended to underestimate the repressive capacity of the 'pacifist' English, Dutch and American states, at times appearing to think that socialism could be achieved in these countries by peaceful and electoral means alone. The result was that Marx never produced any coherent or comparative account of the political structures of bourgeois class power at all. There is a notable disjuncture between his early politico-philosophical writings and his later economic writings.

(ii) Allied to this failure seems to have been an incomprehension of much of the nature of the later epoch through which he lived. Although Marx was alone in his life-time in understanding the economic dynamism of the capitalist mode of production after 1850, which was to transform the world, he seems never to have registered the great shift in the international state system that accompanied it. The defeats of

1848 appear to have convinced Marx that bourgeois revolutions could no longer occur, because of the fear that capital now everywhere had of labour (hence the betrayals in France and Germany of that year). In fact, the rest of his life witnessed a succession of triumphant capitalist revolutions in Germany, Italy, the USA, Japan and elsewhere. These all occurred under the banner of nationalism, not of democracy. Marx assumed that capitalism would progressively mitigate and annul nationality in a new universalism: in fact, its development summoned and reinforced nationalism. His inability to perceive this resulted in a series of grave political mistakes during the 1850s and 1860s, when the major dramas of European politics were all interconnected with nationalist struggles. Hence his hostility to the Risorgimento in Italy, his neglect of Bismarckism in Germany, his adulation of Lincoln in the USA, and his approval of Ottomanism in the Balkans (the latter determined by the other 'anachronistic' preoccupation of 1848, his fear of Russia). A central theoretical silence on the character of nations and nationalisms was left, with very damaging consequences, to later generations of socialists.

(iii) The economic architecture of *Capital* itself, Marx's greatest achievement, is not immune to a number of possible doubts. The most insistent of these concern the very theory of value advanced by Marx. Apart from the difficulties associated with his exclusion of scarcity as a determinant (cf. Ricardo), there is the problem of the dating of the labour inputs themselves (cf. Sraffa), and above all the troubling difficulty so far of converting the latter into prices as a quantifiable medium (in contradiction with the normal canons of scientificity, and the conventional comparisons of the discovery of surplus-value with that of oxygen). Another uneasy aspect of the whole theory of value is the distinction between productive and unproductive labour itself, which although essential to it, has never yet been codified theoretically or established empirically by Marx or his successors. The most hazardous conclusions that the system of *Capital* yielded were the general theorem of the falling rate of profit, and the tenet of an ever-increasing class polarization between bourgeoisie and proletariat. Neither has yet been adequately substantiated. The first implied an economic breakdown of capitalism by its inner mechanisms; the second a social breakdown by way – if not of an immiseration of the proletariat

– of an ultimate absolute preponderance of a vast industrial working class of productive labourers over a tiny bourgeoisie, with few or no intermediary groups. The very absence of any political theory proper in the late Marx may thus be logically related to a latent catastrophism in his economic theory, which rendered the development of the former redundant.

The case of Lenin presents another set of problems, because unlike Marx or Engels, Lenin was not only the author of an original theory but the architect of a political practice that eventually organized a socialist revolution and created a proletarian state. The relations between his theory and practice are thus as important as the relations between his theoretical theses themselves. The main problems that his life and work appear to pose are those which concern proletarian democracy (in party and state), and bourgeois democracy (in West and East).

(i) Lenin's initial theory of an ultra-centralized, neo-jacobin party in *What is to be Done?* was explicitly premised on the distinction between conditions of clandestinity in autocratic Russia and legality in constitutionalist Germany. It was somewhat adjusted to the mass revolts that occurred during the revolution of 1905–6, but never officially revised or modified by Lenin. In 1917, the re-emergence of Soviets in Russia persuaded Lenin that workers' councils were the necessary revolutionary form of proletarian power, by contrast with the universal forms of capitalist power in Europe, and he produced the first real development of Marxist political theory by his famous interpretation of them in *State and Revolution.* However, Lenin neither then nor later ever linked or integrated his doctrine of the party with his account of the soviets, in Russia or elsewhere. His texts on the former make no mention of the latter, his texts on the latter are silent on the former. The result was to permit an extremely swift reversion from the radical soviet democratism of *State and Revolution* to the radical party authoritarianism of the actual Russian State after the onset of the Civil War. Lenin's speeches after the Civil War register the decline of the soviets, but without sustained concern or serious regret. His ultimate remedies for a revival of proletarian democracy against the encroachments of a chauvinist bureaucracy in the USSR merely propose limited internal changes within the party, not within the class or country: there is no allusion to soviets in his political will. The theoretical failure involved here may be related to the practical mistakes committed by Lenin and the Bolsheviks during and after the Civil War, in the exercise and justification of a political repression of opposition that will probably prove often to have been unnecessary and retrograde, when Marxist historians have honestly studied it.

(ii) Lenin started his career by acknowledging the fundamental historical distinction between Western and Eastern Europe in *What is to be Done?*. At various later dates (especially in *Left-Wing Communism*), he alluded to it again. But he never seriously made it an object of Marxist political reflection as such. It is notable that perhaps his greatest work, *State and Revolution*, is wholly generic in its discussion of the bourgeois state – which could be anywhere in the world from the way in which he treats it. In fact, the Russian state which had just been eliminated by the February Revolution was categorically distinct from the German, French, English or American states with which the quotations from Marx and Engels on which Lenin relied had been concerned. By failing to delimit a feudal autocracy unequivocally from bourgeois democracy, Lenin involuntarily permitted a constant confusion among later Marxists, that was effectively to prevent them from ever developing a cogent revolutionary strategy in the West. This could only have been done on the basis of a direct and systematic theory of the representative bourgeois-democratic state in the advanced capitalist countries and the specific combinations of its machinery of consent and coercion, which were foreign to Tsarism. The practical consequence of this theoretical blockage was the inability of the Third International, founded and guided by Lenin, to achieve any mass implantation in the greatest centres of modern imperialism in the twenties – the Anglo-Saxon world of England and USA. Another type of party and another type of strategy were needed in these societies, and were not invented. Lenin's economic work on *Imperialism*, at the time when it was written (1916) a considerable advance, nevertheless remained largely descriptive and after the War tended to suggest an incapacity of modern capitalism to recover from its disasters that found official formulation in numerous Comintern documents. Once again, a tacit economic catastrophism thus functioned to dispense socialist militants from the difficult work of developing a political theory of the State structures with which they had to contend in the West.

Little serious theoretical assessment of Trotsky's work has yet been made. Deutscher's biography, probably the most widely read life of any revolutionary, has curiously not been accompanied or succeeded by any comparably systematic study of Trotsky's ideas – perhaps partly because its very merits have concealed the necessity for this. Closer in time to the political polemics of today than that of the other theorists of the classical tradition, Trotsky's work needs a dispassionate and honest analysis of a type it has not so far generally received. The central difficulties it poses seem to be these.

(i) The notion of 'permanent revolution' was advanced by Trotsky to explain and predict the course of the Russian Revolution. It proved accurate. No bourgeois revolution occurred in Russia; no intermediate capitalist stabilization developed; a working-class insurrection installed a proletarian state within a few months of the end of Tsarism; and this state failed to construct socialism once it was isolated in a single country. However, after 1924, Trotsky generalized his schema of the Russian Revolution to include the entire colonial and ex-colonial world, declaring that henceforward there could be no successful bourgeois revolution in any backward country, and no stabilized capitalist phase of development prior to a proletarian revolution. The two main accomplishments always cited as impossible for any colonial bourgeoisie were the achievement of national independence and a solution of the agrarian question. Post-war historical experience was to be more ambiguous. The example of the Algerian Revolution appears to contradict the former assessment; the case of the Bolivian Revolution the latter. A third criterion, not so often mentioned, was the establishment of representative (parliamentary) democracy: thirty years of the Indian Union suggests that this too may be possible. Secondary lines of defence might argue that no ex-colonial country has ever met all three criteria, or that true independence, agrarian settlement and democracy have never been gained in any country, because of the role of imperialism, usury and corruption in them. But any undue extension of the criteria for a bourgeois revolution of this sort either tends to make the theory of permanent revolution itself into a tautology (only socialism can by definition subtract a country completely from the world market, or solve all the problems of a peasantry), or demands credentials of it which would never have been met by the advanced capitalist countries themselves (which took centuries to achieve bourgeois democracy, for example, with many regressions similar to those of contemporary India). The axiom of 'permanent revolution' must therefore be deemed so far unproven as a general theory. Its difficulties could perhaps have been surmised from its literal derivation from a text of Marx in 1850. Canonical fidelity to Marx of this kind is unlikely ever to be a guarantee of scientific accuracy.

(ii) Trotsky's writings on fascism represent the only direct and developed analysis of a modern capitalist state in the whole of classical Marxism. Superior in quality to anything in Lenin, they nevertheless deal with what has proved to be an atypical form of bourgeois state in the twentieth century, however historically momentous its appearance was at the time. To theorize the specificity of the fascist state as the most deadly enemy to any working class, Trotsky had, of course, to provide elements of a counter-theory of the bourgeois-democratic state, to establish the contrast between the two. There is thus more of substance on bourgeois democracy in his writings than in those of any of his predecessors. However, Trotsky never developed a systematic account of it. The lack of such a theory then seems to have had determinate effects on his political judgements after the victory of Nazism. In particular, whereas his essays on Germany emphasized the imperative need to win the petty-bourgeoisie to an alliance with the working class (citing the example of the bloc against Kornilov in Russia), his essays on the Popular Front in France dismissed the traditional organization of the local petty-bourgeoisie, the Radical Party, as merely a party of 'democratic imperialism' that must on principle be excluded from any anti-fascist alliance. The same shift is evident in his articles on the Civil War in Spain, although with some qualifications and corrections. Then, at the start of the Second World War, Trotsky condemned the international conflict as merely an inter-imperialist repetition of the First World War, in which the working class should opt for neither side – despite the fascist character of the one and the bourgeois-democratic character of the other. This position was justified by an assertion that since the whole imperialist world was deteriorating towards economic disaster in the thirties anyway, the distinction between the two forms of capitalist state had ceased to be of practical importance for the working class. The errors of this theoretical evolution seem evident. Trotsky's own earlier writings on Germany are the best refutation of his later writings on the War. Once the USSR was attacked by Germany, of course, Trotsky would have altered his position on the world conflict. But the economic catastrophism which seems to have motivated the errors of his final phase was a constant of the Third International from Lenin onwards, and had its ultimate authority, as we have seen, in Marx.

(iii) Trotsky was the first Marxist to develop a theory of the bureaucratization of a workers' state. His account of the USSR in the thirties remains a masterly achievement, by any standards. However, all the implications and paradoxes of the notion of a 'workers' state' that systematically repressed and exploited the working class were, perhaps inevitably, never explored by him. In particular, the theory as he bequeathed it was not likely to predict or explain the emergence of new states of this type other than Russia, where there was either no comparable industrial proletariat (China) or no comparable social revolution from below (Eastern Europe), and where yet an obviously similar historical system was created – without any prior degeneration. Later polemics over the extension of the notion of 'Stalinism' were to reflect this difficulty. A further problem in Trotsky's general theory of the nature of a bureaucratized workers' state was to be posed by his thesis that a coercive 'political revolution' was indispensable to restore proletarian democracy where it had been abolished by a usurper caste of officials. This prospect has so far been repeatedly vindicated by developments in the USSR, against the hopes of those like Deutscher who believed in the possibility of a gradual and peaceful reform of bureaucratic rule from above. But its premise was evidently the pre-existence of an original proletarian democracy that had been confiscated and so could be recovered in an immediate political revolt. In China, Vietnam and Cuba, however, the notion of a 'political revolution' has appeared historically much less obviously persuasive, because of the lack of any initial soviets to restore. In other words, in these countries the difficult question of 'dating' the period when a political revolution could be deemed a timely and non-utopian objective was posed.

Trotsky left few scenarios of how this might occur even in Russia. There has been virtually no discussion of how it could or should be accomplished in China or Cuba since. Some of the most important problems involved in any notion of a 'workers' state' or 'political revolution' thus remained unsolved.

These, then, are some of the canonical problems posed by any study of the classical literature of historical materialism. To register them is in no way to fail in respect for the greatest of its thinkers. It would be absurd to imagine that Marx or Lenin or Trotsky could have success-fully solved all the problems of their life-times – let alone those which emerged after them. That Marx did not decipher the enigma of national-ism, that Lenin did not elucidate the sway of bourgeois democracy, that Trotsky did not predict revolutions without soviets, is occasion neither for surprise nor for censure. The scale of their achievements is not diminished by any list of their omissions or mistakes. Indeed, since the tradition they represent was always concerned with political and economic structures in a way that Western Marxism, with its typically philosophical orientation, was not, the same issues re-emerge practically as universal problems before any socialist militant in the contemporary world. We have seen how numerous and insistent these are, by now. What is the constitutive nature of bourgeois democracy? What is the function and future of the nation-state? What is the real character of imperialism as a system? What is the historical meaning of a workers' state without workers' democracy? How can a socialist revolution be made in the advanced capitalist countries? How can internationalism be made a genuine practice, not merely a pious ideal? How can the fate of previous revolutions in comparable conditions be avoided in the ex-colonial countries? How can established systems of bureaucratic privilege and oppression be attacked and abolished? What would be the structure of an authentic socialist democracy? These are the great unanswered problems that form the most urgent agenda for Marxist theory today.

Index